The Adven
A new adapt

Lee Hall's theatre work inclu ... enner's
Leonce and Lena (Gate Theatre), ... ala and His
Man Matti (The Right Size/Alme ... verse and West
End), *Mother Courage and Her Children* (Shared Experience),
Cooking with Elvis (Edinburgh Festival and Whitehall
Theatre), *A Servant to Two Masters* (RSC/Young Vic) and the
stage adaptation of his award-winning radio play, *Spoonface
Steinberg* (Duke of York's). He wrote the screenplay for *Billy
Elliot* and is filming an adaptation of another of his prize-
winning radio plays, *I Love You Jimmy Spud*. His television
work includes *Ted and Alice*, *The Student Prince* and *Spoonface
Steinberg*.

The Adventures of Pinocchio

by

Carlo Collodi

a new adaptation by

Lee Hall

Methuen

Published by Methuen 2000

1 3 5 7 9 10 8 6 4 2

First published in 2000 by Methuen Publishing Limited
215 Vauxhall Bridge Road, London SW1V 1EJ

Methuen Publishing Limited Reg. No. 3543167

ISBN 0 413 76720 5

Typeset by SX Composing DTP, Rayleigh, Essex
Printed and bound in Great Britain by
Cox & Wyman Ltd, Reading, Berkshire

Introduction

I was asked to provide a structure and some dialogue for a production of *Pinocchio* by my good friend Marcello Magni. Having grown up with *Pinocchio* in its film, theatrical and literary versions in Italy, Marcello had all sorts of ideas about producing the play. He wanted to use clowning, puppetry – all sorts of devices from the improvisatory tradition of *commedia dell'arte*.

We held a workshop with a number of actors who contributed wonderful things to the pool of ideas and I went away to structure the material into something Marcello could use as a basis for a production. However, when I read and re-read Collodi's wonderful and mysterious text I ended up writing something which resembles a 'play' much more than I had anticipated. However, anyone approaching this script with thoughts of producing it in the theatre should take it with a pinch of salt. I see this text as a pool of suggestions rather than a set of instructions. It should be cut, expanded, messed about and improvised on to suit the needs and strengths of all those involved. It is more faithful to Collodi's book than any of the other version I have seen, but inevitably it takes some liberties. Anyone considering working on this version of *Pinocchio* should use my script as a companion piece, a sort of 'guide' to Collodi's novel. Things which seem sketchy and unclear in these pages have all their background notes in Collodi's book. So what you have here is a handbook to making a play of *Pinocchio*. This is what we had when we went into rehearsals and it seems to make more sense to publish this, rather than a word for word account of what we will end up with in the theatre piece, as it is very much in the spirit of our endeavour that each version of *Pinocchio* should be an individual and personal response to Collodi's book. Use and abuse this text as you will.

Lee Hall

The Adventures of Pinocchio

Lee Hall's dramatisation of *The Adventures of Pinocchio* premiered at the Lyric Theatre Hammersmith on 24 November 2000. The cast was as follows:

Pinocchio	Eric Mallet
Geppetto, Puppetmaster, Owl	Paul Hunter
Master Cherry, Lampwick,	
Raven, Puppets	Jan Knightley
Fox, Pantaloon, Teacher, Carabiniere	Harry Gostelow
Cat, Harlequin, Cricket, Ringmaster	Linda Kerr Scott
Girl, Inn Keeper	Jules Melvin
Rabbit of Death	Phuong Nguyen

Director Marcello Magni
Designer Rae Smith
Lighting Paul Anderson
Composer Gerard McBurney
Associate director Jan Willem Van Den Bosch
Puppetry director Sue Buckmaster
Musical director Phuong Nguyen

Characters
Geppetto; Master Cherry; Pinocchio; Carabiniere; Man; Cricket; Harlequin; Pantaloon; Puppetmaster; Lady Puppet; Fox; Cat; Waiter; Girl; Owl; Raven; Rabbit of Death; Bird; Boy; Lampwick; Teacher; Donkey

Notes
There is an idea that the Girl plays at being dead/a Mummy/etc. So all the maternal figures are all conjured up in a childish game. We wanted to give the actress some through-line, as the appearances of the Blue Lady in the book are very disparate. We wanted to find a way of making these feminine apparitions tangible rather than ghost-like. Having Pinocchio and the Girl role-play seemed to accentuate the real loss and wish-fulfilment, as well as the fantastical elements.

A **lazzo** is an improvised bravura flourish, a piece of farce or comic dialogue in the tradition of the *commedia dell'arte*.

Act One

THE BLOCK OF WOOD

As the audience come in the stage is bare apart from a block of wood in a spotlight. Eventually the house lights come down and a cold wind whistles across the stage – perhaps played by the accordion.
Geppetto *comes on to the stage. He is freezing cold. The wind whistles. He wraps his coat more firmly around his shoulders and is muttering to himself, almost as if his teeth are chattering dementedly with the cold and he is keeping himself sane with his own story.*

Geppetto   Once upon a time . . . once upon a time . . . once upon a time . . . there was a Prince . . . no . . . once upon a time there was a frog . . . no . . . once upon a time there was . . .

Geppetto *spots the block of wood.*

Geppetto (*incredibly pleased with himself*)   Once upon a time there was a block of wood.

He smiles, turns (as if to God) and kisses his fingers in a gesture of thanks for having found it. Just as his back is turned **Master Cherry** *comes on. Without a by your leave he picks up the piece of wood and starts to make off with it.* **Geppetto** *turns round and sees* **Master Cherry** *and the wood disappearing.*

Geppetto   Wait!

Master Cherry *stops.*

Geppetto   That's my piece of wood.

Master Cherry   What do you mean, it's your piece of wood?

Geppetto   I was walking through the wood and there was a piece of wood and then I went (*Imitates his kiss.*) and then you were off with it.

Master Cherry   Well, if it's your piece of wood, I suppose it's got your name on it.

Master Cherry *gives* **Geppetto** *the piece of wood to show him where his name is on it. As* **Geppetto** *looks helplessly at the wood, it hits him on the nose.*

Geppetto (*to* **Master Cherry**)   There's no need for that!

Master Cherry   For what?

Master Cherry *grabs the wood back. It hits him on the head.*

Master Cherry   Now if you're going to get nasty about it.

Geppetto   About what?

The wood hits **Master Cherry** *again.*

Master Cherry   You ungrateful swine, I was going to let you have it.

Master Cherry *and* **Geppetto** *fight. After a while they stop out of pure exhaustion. They realise they are now wearing each other's wigs and swap them rather embarrassedly. They get up calmly.*

Geppetto   No hard feelings then.

Master Cherry   No hard feelings.

Master Cherry *leaves.*

THE BIRTH OF PINOCCHIO

Lighting change: we are in **Geppetto's** *hovel.*

Geppetto *is freezing.*

Geppetto   That's better. Now to make a nice warm fire.

He goes to get his matches. The wood squeals in horror. He turns to see what is making the noise. Nothing.

I must have my matches somewhere.

Another squeal. **Geppetto** *turns round. He looks at the nose on the wood.*

Damn, the matches, I know. I won't make a fire after all. I know what I'll do I'll make a puppet. A sort of lovely little son and we'll go begging on the corner and make ourselves enough money for a fire every day.

He goes to find his tools.

Yes, a little companion to keep me company in my old age. Oh, yes, what a stroke of genius. We'll make ourselves a fortune.

He makes the puppet. The puppet starts to come to life, unbeknown to **Geppetto**. *The nose grows and grows.* **Geppetto** *cuts it back. The puppet kicks him.* **Geppetto** *has no idea what's going on. He gets spooked. The puppet grabs* **Geppetto**'s *wig, etc. Finally, when* **Geppetto** *realises* **Pinocchio** *has come to life . . .*

Geppetto   You're alive!

Pinocchio   Am I?

Geppetto   My sweet little son.

Pinocchio *kicks* **Geppetto**.

Geppetto   Ow! You're a bad little puppet. You aren't even finished and you're kicking me black and blue. You'll have to learn to respect your father.

Pinocchio   I do respect my father.

Pinocchio *kicks* **Geppetto** *again.*

Geppetto   Ow!

Geppetto *holds on to his leg as* **Pinocchio** *runs away. But as he can't walk properly he falls all over the place.*

Geppetto   You're a bad, bad little Pinocchio.

Pinocchio *is getting the hang of running and escapes* **Geppetto**'s *grip.*

Geppetto   Come here to your daddy at once!

Pinocchio *starts running around in circles, faster and faster.*

Geppetto   Pinocchio. Calm down!

Geppetto *tries to catch him but he is simply too slow.* **Pinocchio** *jumps over his head and runs off into the street.*

Geppetto   Stop! Pinocchio! Pinocchio!

Pinocchio *is off – perhaps running round the auditorium.*

Geppetto   Stop! Pinocchio! Somebody catch that puppet.

Pinocchio *is running wildly, exhilarated by the movement.*

Pinocchio   Wheeeeeeeeeeeeeeeeeeeeeeeeeeeeeeeeee!!!!!!!!!!

PINOCCHIO AND THE POLICEMAN

Geppetto *chases* **Pinocchio**. **Pinocchio** *enjoys the chase and is confident he cannot be stopped when he runs into a* **Carabiniere** *who grabs* **Pinocchio** *by the nose.* **Pinocchio**'s *legs keep going and he only gradually realises he is not now running and has been caught.*

Carabiniere   Hello, hello, hello. What's all this, then?

Pinocchio *looks up at the* **Carabiniere** *in fear.* **Geppetto** *has now caught up, sweating and exhausted.*

Geppetto   Pinocchio. I'll box your wooden ears for running away like that.

Pinocchio   But I haven't got any ears.

Geppetto   Less of your cheek, you hear! (*To* **Carabiniere**.) Terribly sorry, Officer, he's normally very well behaved. Aren't you?

Pinocchio *blows a raspberry.*

Geppetto   You just wait till I get you home. (*He smiles at the* **Carabiniere**.) Don't worry, Officer, everything's under control. Thanks very much for your help.

Pinocchio (*of the* **Carabiniere**)   What an ugly man.

Geppetto *takes* **Pinocchio**'s *hand, but* **Pinocchio** *collapses to the ground and refuses to move.* **Geppetto** *smiles at the* **Carabiniere** – *but talks to* **Pinocchio** *through the side of his mouth.*

Geppetto   Get up.

Pinocchio   I don't want to go home.

Geppetto   Get up, you little workey ticket.

Pinocchio   I want to stay here.

Geppetto *tries to pull* **Pinocchio** *away but he won't budge.*

Geppetto   Stop messing around.

The **Carabiniere** *looks at them suspiciously.*

Carabiniere   Are you sure this little chap is yours?

Geppetto   Of course he's mine.

Geppetto *gives* **Pinocchio** *one last yank but* **Geppetto** *is pulled to the ground. A group of people gather.*

Person 1   Look at that poor little puppet.

Person 2   I wouldn't leave him with that awful Geppetto. God knows what he'll do to him when he gets home.

Geppetto   I won't do anything to him. He's just a puppet.

Geppetto *is struggling to get* **Pinocchio** *to his feet. The* **Carabiniere** *intervenes.*

Carabiniere   All right, that's enough now. I'm not tolerating that kind of nonsense. (*To* **Pinocchio**.) You – hop it. And you (*To* **Geppetto**.) can come with me.

Pinocchio *squeals with glee and starts dancing around. Poor* **Geppetto** *is dragged off by the* **Carabiniere**. *He looks back at* **Pinocchio**. *There are tears in his eyes.*

Geppetto (*shouts*)   Pinocchio! After everything I've done for you.

Pinocchio *is oblivious to* **Geppetto***'s grief and waves bye-bye as if nothing is wrong.*

PINOCCHIO ON HIS OWN

Pinocchio *is now on his own. And jumps and leaps around the stage. He stops for a second and hears a groan. He looks round. There is another groan. He looks for it. Finally he realises the groan came from his own stomach and he is, in fact, hungry.*

Pinocchio   Oh! I'm hungry!

He suddenly realises **Geppetto** *would provide for him.*

Pinocchio   Wait. Geppetto.

He looks out into the distance but it's too late. His stomach rumbles again.

Pinocchio   Oh, no. Sssssssshhhh.

Pinocchio *tries to make his stomach quiet. The weather turns and it starts to snow – he realises it is night, and he is cold and alone.*

Pinocchio   Food . . . (*He goes to the door of a house and knocks.*) Hello, hello. Is there anyone there?

A **Man** *comes to the door.*

Pinocchio   Excuse me, sir. I am a puppet all alone in the world and terribly hungry for some food. Do you have anything? Anything at all you could spare me?

Man   Yeah. You just wait there, sunshine.

Pinocchio *is overjoyed and dances in appreciation. The* **Man** *reappears and throws a bucket of water over him.*

Man   Now get off out of it, you scrounging mongrel, and never darken our doors again.

Pinocchio *is shocked and tearful. It is snowing heavily. He shivers and rattles.*

Pinocchio   I want to go home. I want to go home.

He sees that **Geppetto**'s *house is nearby – maybe a sign saying* GEPPETTO'S HOUSE.

Pinocchio   Oh! Look. (*He shivers and makes his way indoors.*)

PINOCCHIO AND THE CRICKET

Inside **Geppetto**'s *hovel.*

Pinocchio *comes in. It is cold and dark.* **Pinocchio** *is cold and hungry. He starts to look for some food.*

Pinocchio   Food. Food. There must be something to eat.

He looks in all the most inappropriate places. The **Cricket** *is watching him.*

Cricket   Tut-tut-tut.

Pinocchio *looks around, shocked/spooked.*

Pinocchio   Who said that?

Cricket   Tut-tut. Who do you think said that? It is I.

Pinocchio *looks around for the voice and finally sees the* **Cricket**.

Pinocchio   Who are you?

Cricket   I'm the talking Cricket, of course.

Pinocchio   What are you doing here?

Cricket   What do you think I'm doing here? I live here. I've lived here for the last hundred years, I'll have you know.

Pinocchio   Well do me a favour, long-legs. Get out of it; this is my room now.

Cricket   Excuse me, young man, I will certainly not 'get out of it'. I've every mind to teach you a lesson.

Pinocchio   Well, you'd better hurry up. I've got food to find.

Cricket   Well, if children obeyed their elders and didn't go running off without a by your leave they might have some food, mightn't they. You'll be sorry one day, mark my words.

Pinocchio   Oh, give it a rest, you overgrown tick. Listen, I'm going to get something to eat, have a little sleep and I'll be out of here by morning. I'm not sticking around in this dump so the old fool can send me to school.

Cricket   You should go to school. It'd do you good.

Pinocchio   Well, let me tell you what I'm going to study. Jumping around, climbing up trees and lazing about. Got it, you little woodlouse?

Cricket   Well, if you want to be a complete jackass you're going the right way about it.

Pinocchio   Shut up, you stupid cockroach.

Cricket   You'll end up in prison.

Pinocchio   I'm warning you, you sanctimonious little flea.

Cricket   Flea! I'm a cricket. You ignorant piece of wood.

Pinocchio   That's it.

Pinocchio *picks up a mallet and squashes the* **Cricket** *with one hit.* **Pinocchio** *doesn't really understand what he's done. He goes to the squashed creature. He tentatively touches it. It is dead. He prods it. He is puzzled. Then his stomach rumbles. He forgets the* **Cricket**.

Pinocchio   Food.

He carries on looking for food. Eventually in the corner of the room he finds a nest. He looks inside it and brings out an egg. He is delighted. He is extremely careful with it. He salivates. He goes to eat it and realises he should cook it. He gets a pan and takes it to the fireplace. After some trying he realises the fire is painted so he improvises some kindling on the floor. He lights the fire and prepares the pan. He makes an elaborate show of the cookery preparations. He heats the pan and *when everything is ready to go he carefully gets the egg. He licks his lips and cracks it open. A **Bird** flies out.*

Bird   Thanks a lot, matey. I'll be seeing you.

It flies off. **Pinocchio** *is amazed. He tries to catch the **Bird** but it's too late.*

Pinocchio   Oh, no.

Pinocchio *looks worn out, disappointed and dejected. He yawns. At least there is the warmth of the fire. He warms his hands. Yawns again, then falls asleep with his feet resting firmly in the flames. He sleeps, snoring away. His feet start to burn. He turns – we think he'll wake up – but he carries on sleeping. His feet burn off. He sleeps on. Finally, there is a knock on the door.* **Pinocchio** *doesn't stir. Another knock. He wakes at the noise. He is oblivious to the fact that he has no feet. Another knock.*

Pinocchio   Who is it?

Geppetto   It's me, Geppetto.

Pinocchio *wakes up jubilantly, leaps to his feet and falls with a crash.*

Geppetto   Open the door.

Pinocchio *tries to get up but falls back down.*

Geppetto   Open the door, Pinocchio.

Pinocchio   I can't. (*He gets up and falls again.*) I've got no feet.

Geppetto   I'm warning you. Stop messing about.

Pinocchio   Someone's eaten my feet.

Geppetto   Don't be ridiculous. Who would eat your feet?

Pinocchio   A cat has eaten my feet.

Geppetto   Open this door at once, Pinocchio.

Pinocchio *is rolling around on the ground.*

Pinocchio   Help. I'm disabled. I'll have to walk on my knees for the rest of my life.

He walks around on his knees. He can't reach the door handle.

Geppetto   Listen, when I get in there I'm going to give you what for, do you understand?

GEPPETTO HELPS PINOCCHIO

Geppetto *appears at the window and with great difficulty climbs through. He brushes himself down, then turns to* **Pinocchio***, who is weeping on the floor.*

Geppetto   Right!

Geppetto *sees* **Pinocchio** *and is mortified.*

Geppetto   Pinocchio.

Geppetto *rushes to* **Pinocchio** *and picks him up.* **Geppetto** *starts to cry.*

Geppetto   Pinocchio. How did this happen?

Pinocchio   I don't know. I was running around and then it was snowing and then I asked for some food and then a man threw some water on me and then I saw the talking cricket and then I squashed him with a hammer and then I tried to cook an egg and it flew away and said 'bye-bye, matey' and then my feet fell off.

Pinocchio *begins to wail. The more* **Geppetto** *tries to console him the louder and more uncontrollable* **Pinocchio***'s cries become.*

Geppetto   It's all right. Calm down. I'll make you some new feet. It's all right.

Pinocchio *is inconsolable.*

Geppetto   Sh. (*Has an idea.*) Why don't you have this pear?

Geppetto *brings out a mangy pear.* **Pinocchio** *stops crying at once and is the picture of content.*

Geppetto   I was saving it for my supper.

Geppetto *rubs it on his jacket and presents it with a flourish to* **Pinocchio**. *We see* **Geppetto** *is starving too but is delighted that* **Pinocchio** *seems so happy.* **Pinocchio** *takes it, then gives it back.*

Geppetto   What's the matter?

Pinocchio   Peel it for me.

Geppetto   Peel it! There'll be nothing left.

Pinocchio   Listen, if you want me to eat it, you have to peel it first. You don't expect me to eat the skin.

Geppetto   All right, but you'll have to learn not to be so pernickety.

Geppetto *peels the pear and saves the peel for himself. He proudly presents* **Pinocchio** *with the pear.* **Pinocchio** *hands it back.*

Pinocchio   Take the core out.

Geppetto   Pinocchio. You shouldn't be so fussy. This is the first bit of fruit I've had in weeks.

Geppetto *carves out the core and gives the rest of the pear to* **Pinocchio**. **Pinocchio** *gobbles it down in one, then burps. He looks at* **Geppetto**, *who is carefully saving the core.*

Pinocchio   What are you doing?

Geppetto   I'm saving it for later. It'll do for my lunch.

Pinocchio *raises his eyes in disgust. He swings his leg.*

Pinocchio   I'm still hungry.

Geppetto   But I haven't got anything else.

Pinocchio *looks disappointed. He thinks for a moment.*

Pinocchio   What about the peelings?

Geppetto   I thought you didn't want them?

Pinocchio   What do you want me to do? Starve?

Geppetto *gives* **Pinocchio** *the peelings.*

Pinocchio Beggars can't be choosers.

Pinocchio *makes a big deal of being repulsed by the bitter peel, then eats it down in one mouthful.*

Pinocchio That's better.

Geppetto I told you not to be too fussy.

Pinocchio Give it a rest, Pop. What about my feet?

Geppetto Why should I make you new feet if you're only going to run away?

Pinocchio I won't run away. Promise. I'll be a good little puppet and do exactly as I'm told.

Geppetto That's what they all say.

Pinocchio I mean it. Honest. I promise I'll go to school and study and learn a trade and everything. You'll be so proud of me and my feet, and I'll look after you in old age.

Geppetto's *eyes fill with tears.*

Pinocchio Honest, Father.

Pinocchio *is laying on the sincerity very thick.* **Geppetto** *is moved and makes* **Pinocchio** *new feet.*

Pinocchio I'll be good as gold, Dad.

Geppetto *finishes the mending.*

Geppetto There you go.

Pinocchio *jumps to his feet and dances around extravagantly.*

Pinocchio Yippee! Thank you, thank you. And to pay you back for all your kindness, I'm going to go to school right away. Well, as soon as you get me some clothes.

Geppetto But we haven't got any money.

Pinocchio You don't expect me to go naked, do you?

Geppetto *sighs and makes* **Pinocchio** *some clothes.*

Geppetto   Remember, it's not the clothes that make a gentleman, it's how clean they are.

Pinocchio   Thank you, thank you, Father. All I need now is a book.

Geppetto   A book?

Pinocchio   You can't expect me to go to school without a book. I need an ABC.

Geppetto   I don't think you understand. We have no money at all.

Pinocchio *looks at* **Geppetto**. *He realises the desperation of* **Geppetto**. **Pinocchio** *is crestfallen. He understands their poverty. Neither of them can speak. Then* **Geppetto** *has an idea.*

Geppetto   Wait here.

GEPPETTO SWAPS HIS COAT FOR A BOOK

Geppetto *gets his jacket, wraps up against the snow and goes out.* **Pinocchio** *examines his new clothes.*

Pinocchio   Oh, I will go to school and learn everything and be the very best student that ever lived and then I will become rich and then I will do something else. Oh, what a wonderful world this has turned out to be.

Geppetto *comes back without his jacket, but with a book in his hands. He gives* **Pinocchio** *the book proudly.* **Pinocchio** *is overjoyed.*

Pinocchio   Hooray! Hooray! (*He kisses the book.*) But I don't understand. What happened to your jacket?

Geppetto   I sold it.

Pinocchio   Why did you sell it?

Geppetto   It made me too hot.

Pinocchio *realises what* **Geppetto** *has done. He leaps at his father and kisses and caresses him.*

Pinocchio   Don't worry, Father, today at school I'll learn to read and write and then learn arithmetic, and then I'll get a job and earn loads of money and buy you a new jacket. What am I saying? I'll buy you a gold jacket with diamond buttons and a silver hat to keep your wig warm.

Geppetto   Look, just be careful. Go straight to school and don't talk to strangers.

Pinocchio   Don't worry. You are the kindest father in the entire world.

Pinocchio *goes out. It's snowing.* **Pinocchio** *turns to* **Geppetto**.

Pinocchio   I think you'd better go inside. You'll get cold.

And with that he goes off.

PINOCCHIO FAILS TO GO TO SCHOOL AS HE
SEES A PUPPET THEATRE

Pinocchio *is skipping off to school. He is happy. It stops snowing and he gleefully makes his way along. (Possible song about going off to school.) As he skips along he suddenly hears a burst of fairground music off stage. He stops. The music stops. He goes off skipping along again. The music starts up again. He stops and listens. This time it carries on. A* **Person** *runs across the stage towards the music.* **Pinocchio** *watches him with interest. The music carries on. Another* **Person** *runs across towards the music.* **Pinocchio** *shouts after him.*

Pinocchio   Hey! Where are you going?

The **Person** *doesn't answer.* **Pinocchio** *looks towards the school. Then towards the music. He goes off towards school, then changes his mind and heads towards the music.*

Outside the Puppet Theatre.

Pinocchio *can hear music and laughter from inside the theatre. A* **Man** *is standing by.* **Pinocchio** *tries to see what is going on. The* **Man** *watches him dismissively.*

Pinocchio   What's going on? What's going on?

Man   What's the matter. Can't you read?

The **Man** *points to the sign.*

Pinocchio   Actually, no. I was just on my way to school to learn.

Man   For your information, Jackass, it says THE MAGIC PUPPET THEATRE.

Pinocchio   Wow. How much does it cost to go in?

Man   Fourpence.

Pinocchio (*thinks*)   Would you lend me fourpence till tomorrow?

Man   Get lost, will you?

Pinocchio   I'd sell you my jacket. (*No luck.*) What about my shoes? (*Nothing doing.*) What about my hat?

Man   It's made of bread.

Pinocchio   Is it?

Man   Look, give me the book and I'll give you fourpence.

Pinocchio *looks very confused. He doesn't want to sell the book. The* **Man** *looks on, knowing he has a hold over* **Pinocchio**. *We hear laughing inside.* **Pinocchio** *finally relents, sells the book and rushes into the theatre with his fourpence.*

THE PUPPET THEATRE

The stage turns into a theatre. Theatrical music. Applause and laughter from the auditorium. Two **Puppets** *appear. They are overacting in a Donald Wolfit fashion.*

Pantaloon   Oh, what is this wretch I see before me? Forsooth, art thou not the villain who hath besmirched my handkerchief?

Harlequin   I am no villain. I did not besmirch your handkerchief.

Harlequin *kicks* **Pantaloon** *up the bum.*

Pantaloon   O thou worthless vermin, thou. Look at what thou hast done. (*Shows the handkerchief.*) I shall unknave thee chin from chops.

Pantaloon *wallops* **Harlequin** *across the face.*

Harlequin   Take that, thou rancorous slave.

Harlequin *retaliates.*

Pantaloon   Thou malodorous pisspot.

Harlequin   Dog breath.

Pantaloon   Thou nappy sniffer.

Harlequin   Cretinous fool.

The insults and punches have descended into an almighty scrap. By this time **Pinocchio** *has entered into the stalls of the auditorium. He makes a lot of fuss climbing over people: ''Scuse me, 'Scuse me.'* **Pinocchio** *makes so much fuss that suddenly* **Pantaloon** *breaks off from the fight and looks into the auditorium.*

Pantaloon   Do I dream or am I awake? Is that not Pinocchio?

Harlequin   Pinocchio!!

Harlequin *looks out into the auditorium.*

Harlequin   By George, I think you're right.

Pantaloon   Thank Thespis, yes, it is our Thespian brother, Pinocchio. Pinocchio! Everybody, it's Pinocchio.

More **Puppets** *run from the wings.* **Pantaloon** *runs to the front of the stage.*

Pantaloon   Come, come to your brothers.

Pinocchio, *excited by the invitation, starts climbing over the seats, eating sweets from children on the way, etc. and generally causing chaos as he makes his way to the stage. The* **Puppets** *haul him up and raise him aloft in happiness.*

Puppets   Pinocchio! Pinocchio!

Pantaloon *kisses* **Pinocchio** *in a flamboyantly theatrical way.*

Pantaloon   How marvellous to see you, my darling boy.

Puppets   Hooray!

General rejoicing. Voices come from the auditorium.

Audience   Hang on a minute. I want my money back . . . Get on with it . . . Get on with the show . . .

The crowd start booing and hissing. **Pantaloon** *comes forward.*

Pantaloon   Be quiet, you philistine creatures. Can't you see we are celebrating?

Pinocchio *is being showered with kisses. Then suddenly the* **Puppetmaster** *appears. All of a sudden the* **Puppets** *fall silent. Everybody quakes in their boots, terrified. The* **Puppetmaster** *addresses* **Pinocchio**.

Puppetmaster   You.

Pinocchio   M-m-m-m-m-me, sir?

Puppetmaster   What do you think you are up to? Creating a riot in my theatre.

Pinocchio   I'm terribly sorry, your most illustrious majesty, sir.

Puppetmaster I can't work in these conditions. The show is cancelled.

Audience I want my money back.

Puppetmaster *shouts into the* **Audience**. *It would scare anyone.*

Puppetmaster Get out of here now, before I eat you for lunch.

Pantaloon But Mr Fire-eater, sir . . .

Puppetmaster I don't want to hear another word out of you, you old ham. I want my supper. There are five sheep on the spit outside, if I were you I'd get a fire started pronto or you'll be playing second spear catcher for the whole of the summer season, understood?

Pantaloon But Mr Fire-eater, sir. Where will I get the firewood?

Puppetmaster Throw him on for a start. He's perfect for tinder.

Pantaloon *and* **Harlequin** *look at one another and gulp.*

Puppetmaster NOW!

Pantaloon *and* **Harlequin** *grab* **Pinocchio**.

Pinocchio Oh, please, Father, help me! I don't want to die. Please! I don't want to die.

Puppetmaster Throw him on the fire.

There are gasps from the other **Puppets**. **Pantaloon** *and* **Harlequin** *are frozen to the spot.*

Pinocchio Please. I don't want to die. I'm just a little puppet. I'm only a day and a half old.

The **Puppetmaster** *listens to* **Pinocchio**'s *pleading.*

Pinocchio Please, give me one little chance. I'll never set foot in another theatre as long as I live.

The **Puppetmaster** *seems to be listening. He sniffles with (we think) anger. The* **Puppets** *cover themselves in anticipation.*

Pinocchio   I'm just a poor little puppet without a friend in the world.

Pinocchio *starts to cry. The* **Puppetmaster** *begins to sneeze.*

Puppetmaster   A . . . a . . . a . . . a . . . a . . . a . . . CHOOOOOOOOO!!!!

A howling wind blows from the **Puppetmaster**'s *sneeze. The* **Puppets** *hold on to their hats etc.*

Pantaloon   Good news, darling. He only ever sneezes when he gets sentimental.

Puppetmaster   A . . . a . . . a . . . a . . . a . . . a . . . a . . . chooooooooo.

Pantaloon   I think you're saved.

The **Puppetmaster** *starts to splutter after his sneeze.*

Puppetmaster   Stop. Stop. Hold everything. I have been touched to the pit of my stomach. Let the little puppet go. No, a pardon has been granted. No longer will this poor creature cook my dinner. Tell me, what about your mother and father? Are they still alive?

Pinocchio   I don't know. I think my father is. But I've never had a mother.

Pantaloon (*aside to* **Pinocchio**)   Don't overdo it.

Puppetmaster   A . . . A . . . A . . . A . . . CHOO!

Pinocchio   Bless you.

Puppetmaster   Come. Come, my poor little puppet. People don't understand me. They think I'm some kind of tyrant, some kind of heartless ogre, but I have all sorts of pressures: business has gone completely out of the window since the Risorgimento. No, under this beard of flax is a heart of gold.

Everybody *relaxes.*

Puppetmaster   Come, come, my little puppet. What was I thinking of sending a poor innocent creature to certain death? Don't worry – we'll just burn one of the company instead.

The **Company** *go into panicked shock.*

Puppetmaster *points at* **Pantaloon**.

Puppetmaster   You'll do. Throw him on the fire.

Harlequin *grabs* **Pantaloon** *reluctantly,* **Pantaloon** *faints.* **Pinocchio** *is horrified. He throws himself at the* **Puppetmaster***'s feet.*

Pinocchio   Signor Fire-eater, sir. Have pity.

Puppetmaster   I am no signor.

Pinocchio   Well, Sir Fire-eater, sir.

Puppetmaster   Sir?

Pinocchio   Well, have pity, your grand, all-seeing, gracious and very handsome excellency, sir.

Puppetmaster   Excellency. I like 'excellency'.

Pinocchio (*aside*)   What terrible breath. (*To* **Puppetmaster**.) Please, your most excellent excellency. The most excellent excellent excellency for all the goodness and grace in this sad and lonely world, please take pity on this poor company of humble puppets. If you burn one of my brothers, sir, you burn me.

The **Puppetmaster** *begins to sniffle.*

Puppetmaster   But you don't understand. How am I going to roast my mutton?

Pinocchio   Well, in that case, I see where my duty lies, your excellency. Come, bind me. Tie me to a stake and burn me in the flames. I will not let one of my brothers die

when I could proudly burn in his place. Take me, sir, I am
yours.

Everybody *is astonished and deeply moved by* **Pinocchio**'*s
speech. There is crying and the sound of a prolonged sneeze.*

Puppetmaster   A...a...a...a...a...a...

Harlequin   Bravo, that puppet! Beautifully delivered.

Puppetmaster   CHOOOOOOOOOOOOOOOO!!!!!!!!!

Puppets (*rejoice*)   Bravo!

Lady Puppet   Perhaps we have our Hamlet?

Puppetmaster   Bravissimo. Bravo, my boy. I am so
deeply moved. Come to me. Let me kiss you.

Pinocchio *goes to the* **Puppetmaster**.

Pantaloon   So, is mercy granted?

Puppetmaster   Of course mercy is granted. How could I
eat after that performance? Tonight I go without supper.
Just get plenty of firewood for tomorrow or I might not be
so lenient.

The **Puppets** *rejoice. They kiss* **Pinocchio**. **Pantaloon** *sits, as
he is overcome with it all.*

Puppetmaster   Tell me, little fellow, what is your
father's name?

Pinocchio   I think he is called Geppetto.

Puppetmaster   And what does he do for a living?

Pinocchio   He's a poor man, sir.

Puppetmaster   How much does he earn, my sad
puppet?

Pinocchio   Not much at all. He had to sell his jacket to
send me to school.

Puppetmaster   Let nobody say I am not a generous man. Here are five gold coins. Take them to him right away. Buy him a new coat and food fit for kings.

Puppetmaster *gives* **Pinocchio** *the money.* **Pinocchio** *reels from the bad breath.*

Pinocchio   I don't know how to thank you.

Puppetmaster   Don't thank me. Make haste. And tell your father he has a remarkable little son. Now go. Go. And whatever you do, take care on the road.

Pinnocchio   Don't worry. I'll go straight home and won't talk to anyone.

Pinocchio *bids a fond farewell to his comrades and waves goodbye.*

Puppetmaster   Right. Now, you horrible lot. Get this place tidied up. We play *Don Giovanni* at seven o'clock sharp.

Pinocchio *goes off. The stage clears.*

PINOCCHIO TRIES TO FIND HIS WAY HOME, BUT GETS INTO TROUBLE.

Geppetto *appears, cold and forlorn. He goes into his hovel and claps his hands to warm himself. He looks around sadly.*

Geppetto   Hello. I'm home. Hello, table. Hello, chair. How're you doing? Good to see you. Hello, fireplace. Hello, the painting of a cauldron. Oh, it's good to be back home.

Geppetto *is evidently very sad and lonely. He glumly fishes in his pocket. He finds some old peelings. He eats them sparingly as the light dims and he fades into darkness.*

The stage clears and from out of the trapdoors come the **Cat** *and the* **Fox.** *They look to see that the coast is clear. The* **Cat** *nonchalantly nibbles something.*

Fox   Well?

Cat   Well what?

Fox Did you get anything?

Cat Any what?

Fox Any food, you imbecile.

Cat Look, I'm not going to give you any if you take that attitude.

Fox You promised. We share everything, remember?

*The **Cat** hands over a tiny vole.*

Fox What's this?

Cat What do you think it is? It's food.

Fox But what is it?

Cat It's a baby vole. Very tasty.

Fox What am I supposed to do with this?

Cat I thought you'd quite like it.

Fox Look, we haven't eaten in three days. I don't want voles. I need proper sustenance. I need a fatted calf, or a dead horse. Not anorexic field mice.

Cat It's not my fault. All the farms have guard dogs.

Fox You're supposed to be a cat. You're supposed to have uncommon powers of deviousness.

Cat Look, if all you're going to do is complain, I'll have that back, thank you very much.

*The **Cat** snatches back the vole.*

Fox Don't be an ass.

Cat What do you mean? I'm a cat.

Fox Look, you blithering idiot, we're going to have to find something soon or we'll waste away.

*They hear someone whistling a tune. The **Cat** and the **Fox** look at each other.*

Fox   Oh, my goodness. I think someone is coming. Just copy what I do and you'll see how to work it like a real professional.

The **Cat** *gives the* **Fox** *a splint and then quickly dons some dark glasses. Then they scuttle off. Enter* **Pinocchio**, *whistling 'I'm in the money'.*

Pinocchio   O Pinocchio, Pinocchio. What a rich puppet you have become.

The **Cat** *and the* **Fox** *appear, the* **Cat** *is blind and the* **Fox** *lame, although he has trouble remembering in which leg.*

Fox   Ah, Pinocchio.

Cat   Ah, Pinocchio.

Pinocchio   How did you know my name?

Fox   How did I know your name?

Cat   How *did* you know his name?

Fox   Why, we are very great friends of your father's.

Cat   Oh, yes. Very great friends of your father's.

Fox (*to* **Cat**)   Look, shut up.

Cat   I'm only doing what I was told.

Fox   For crying out loud, you don't have to repeat every word.

Cat   No. Not every word.

Fox   OK?

Cat   OK.

Pinocchio   So when did you last see my father?

Fox   Ah, a very good question.

Cat   A very good question indeed.

Fox (*to* **Cat**)   Will you shut up? (*To* **Pinocchio**.) Yes, a very fine figure of a man, your father.

Cat   And a very lucky fellow to have such a charming and intelligent son. If you don't mind me saying so.

Fox (*to* **Cat**)   Butt out, Butthead.

Pinocchio   Excuse me. Are you blind?

Fox   As a mole. And I'm unfortunately lame.

Cat   As a mole.

Fox   I lost the use of my leg rescuing a coop full of chickens from a horrendous fire in their hutch near Florence.

Cat   Oh, yes, he's been singed in all sorts of places.

Fox   But enough of us. We want to know about you.

Pinocchio   Well, you're right about my father. He's a very lucky fellow because he's going to be a very rich man.

Fox   Is he, indeed?

Pinocchio   Oh, yes, a very rich man. Because I'm taking him these.

Pinocchio *produces five gold coins. The* **Cat** *and* **Fox** *nearly go into apoplexy.*

Fox   Steady the buffs.

The **Cat** *takes a good hard look, then puts her glasses back on.*

Cat   Really?

Pinocchio   Oh, yes. And I'm going to buy him a golden jacket with diamond buttons and a silver hat. And for myself I'm going to buy a spelling book.

Fox   A spelling book?

Pinocchio   Oh, yes. I want to go to school.

The **Fox** *kicks the* **Cat**, *who winces.*

Fox I beg your pardon?

Pinocchio I want to go to school.

Fox *kicks* **Cat** *again; another wince as if* **Cat** *is reacting to the word school.*

Fox Don't mention that word.

Pinocchio What word? School?

This time **Cat** *gets the game and reacts again.*

Fox Yes, a terrible business. He lost his eyesight through studying too hard.

Pinocchio Oh, my gosh.

Cat And my companion lost his paw because of his compulsion for homework.

Pinocccchio I thought it was through rescuing chickens.

Cat That was his homework.

Fox Oh, yeş. For heaven's sake beware of the iniquitous dangers of education, my lad.

A **Bird** *pops up.*

Bird Take no notice, Pinocchio. Go home to Geppetto.

The **Cat** *grabs the* **Bird** *and stuffs it into its mouth.*

Pinocchio Who said that?

Fox (*burps*) I beg your pardon?

Cat Sorry?

Pinocchio What?

Fox I'm terribly sorry. I haven't got a clue. What's going on?

Pinocchio You just ate a blackbird.

Cat Did I?

Fox   No she didn't, she was just teaching him a lesson. For being ignorant. Perfectly normal.

Cat   No, there's one thing we can't stand and that's ignorance.

Fox (*to* **Cat**)   Shut up. (*To* **Pinocchio**.) For instance, would you believe there are some people who wouldn't even know how to multiply those gold coins?

Cat   Unbelievable.

Fox   It's almost impossible to credit, isn't it? I mean some people wouldn't realise they could be walking around with a hundred.

Cat   A thousand.

Fox   No, a hundred thousand.

Cat   At least.

Fox   It's almost impossible to countenance, don't you think?

Pinocchio   What, you mean I could multiply these gold coins?

Cat   Hahahahahaha.

Fox   Hahahahahaahaa.

Cat *and* **Fox**   Ha ha ha ha ha ha ha!

They stop laughing.

Fox   Of course you can. You mean you've never heard of Dodo-land?

Pinocchio   No. But is it really possible to multiply my gold coins?

Cat   In Dodo-land it's almost impossible to stop.

Fox   Plant a few coins in Dodo-land and they'll be growing on trees.

Pinocchio   Really?

Fox   Would I tell a lie?

Pinocchio *looks at him.*

Fox   What do you reckon?

Pinocchio   Well, I'm not sure . . .

Cat   He won't want to go there, will you?

Fox   Won't he?

Cat   Not when his dad's waiting for him and his five measly coins in dire poverty, with huge expectations of his only son.

Fox (*to* **Cat**)   What on earth are you doing?

Cat (*ignoring* **Fox**)   No, not with those huge expectations.

Pinocchio *thinks hard.*

Pinocchio   You're right. My poor father has been waiting for me and I've been such a bad puppet already. I think I should go straight home immediately. Even though I could go to . . .

Cat   Dodo-land.

Pinocchio   Dodo-land.

Fox   With the Field of Miracles.

Cat   Of course not, because even though it'd be a golden opportunity you're far too sensible.

Fox   No, I think he should go, actually.

Cat   Don't be stupid. His father probably has a pear core waiting for his tea.

Pinocchio   How much did you say I could turn the gold coins into?

Cat   I dunno. A thousand. Two thousand maybe. Hardly worth the bother.

Pinocchio   And all I'd do is go to Dodo-land?

Fox   And bury the money in the Field of Miracles and . . .

Cat   Hey, presto. As many gold pieces as there are ears of corn in June.

Pinocchio   What's June?

Fox   Don't worry about that now.

Pinocchio   Well, that's decided. We'll go there at once and once I have my two thousand coins I'll give a thousand to my father, keep a hundred for me and give you two the rest.

Cat   Us!

Fox   Heaven forfend. You couldn't give any to us.

Cat   Certainly not.

Fox   Because we only work for the benefit of others.

Pinocchio   Oh, you are truly wonderful people. Come on, let's go.

Fox   Are you sure?

Pinocchio   Of course I'm sure.

Fox   It's an awfully long way.

Cat   Perhaps we should stop off for a little sustenance.

Fox   What an excellent idea.

Pinocchio   What an excellent idea. Do you know you have snot on the end of your nose?

*The **Cat** looks indignant, then decides to ignore it.*

Cat   Oh, look! There happens to be a place to eat right here.

The sign for the Red Lobster Inn appears.

Pinocchio   Amazing.

Cat   In we go, there's a good little fellow.

The **Cat** *winks at the* **Fox**. *The* **Fox** *clouts her. They all go into the . . .*

RED LOBSTER INN

Suddenly tables have appeared. The **Fox** *is tucking a napkin into* **Pinocchio**'s *collar.*

Waiter   Can I help you?

Fox   I'm sorry?

Waiter   Can I get you something to eat?

Fox   Oh, heaven forbid.

Cat   Eat? Us?

Fox   Oh, no. I'm afraid my friend here has a severe medical condition that requires a very strict diet and I myself am the complete model of parsimony.

Cat   But perhaps our friend might like something.

They look at **Pinocchio**. *The* **Waiter** *gives him the menu.*

Pinocchio   Well, I don't know. Just something simple, I suppose. What about a walnut and a piece of bread crust? (*He looks sorrowfully at the* **Cat** *and the* **Fox**.) Are you sure you don't want anything?

Cat   No, no, no, no, no, no, no.

Fox   Maybe we'll share whatever you leave.

Pinocchio   Please have something. Really, it's my treat.

Cat   Well in that case, I'd like thirty-five red mullets, with tomato sauce, four portions of tripe à la parmesan, some bread and butter, a tiramisu and a bottle of Barolo.

Waiter   Anything else?

Cat   Well, if you have a turbot or two knocking about, maybe you could drop them in the fryer.

Waiter   Coming right up, sir.

Already food is arriving. **Pinocchio** *sits with his walnut while the* **Cat** *gets stuck into a gargantuan feast.*

Fox (*studying the menu*)   Really, I'm not very hungry at all. But if you insist could I have the hare in sweet and sour sauce. (*We think he's finished.*) Oh, and the capon. (*He's definitely done.*) And the pullets, the calves liver and the leg of lamb. And for my main course could I have the fricassée of partridges, the rabbit in marsala, the frogs' gizzards, the baron of beef, the pheasant stew and the peaches. Could I have the beef rare, please. And a bottle of your sparkling water. No ice.

Waiter   Anything else?

Fox   No. I'm watching my weight.

A carnival of grotesque consumption as **Pinocchio** *picks at his walnut and the* **Cat** *and the* **Fox** *become devouring monsters. They burp and look at* **Pinocchio**.

Fox   Come on. Eat up, lad.

Pinocchio   I can't. I think I've lost my appetite thinking of the Field of Miracles.

Cat   Don't worry, you'll be there soon enough.

The **Fox** *scoffs whatever is left on* **Pinocchio***'s plate.*

Fox   With all this anticipation, I think we should gather our strength together, have a little nap and regroup in a couple of hours.

Cat   An excellent idea. You're looking a bit wan, my lad.

The **Cat** *slaps* **Pinocchio** *on the back.*

Fox   Waiter. Two rooms, please. Our friend would like to be woken at twelve o'clock sharp as we're off to the Field of Miracles.

Waiter   Absolutely. You can count on me.

The **Waiter** *winks at the* **Cat**. *Now the* **Cat** *and* **Fox** *are bamboozling* **Pinocchio** *into his room.*

Cat   That's right. A few hours' kip and we'll be planting our money.

Fox   And Bob's your proverbial uncle.

Cat   So to speak.

Fox   Pleasant dreams.

Pinocchio   But I'm not tired.

The **Cat** *and the* **Fox** *have disappeared.* **Pinocchio** *is on his own. He yawns.*

Pinocchio   I'm not tired at all.

Another yawn.

Pinocchio   At . . . a . . .

Pinocchio *falls fast asleep.*

[*Possible dream sequence.*]

Bang, bang, bang on the door. It's the **Waiter**.

Waiter   All right guv'nor, it's twelve o'clock. Here's the bill.

Pinocchio   What about my companions?

Waiter   They left an hour ago. There was a message that one of the Cat's kittens was taken bad with the chilblains so they had to leave right away. They said they'd meet you in the Field of Miracles.

Pinocchio   Blimey.

Waiter   That's one gold coin, thank you.

Pinocchio   But do you know how to get to the Field of Miracles?

Waiter   Out the door, turn left and follow your nose, squire.

Pinocchio   Thank you.

Waiter   Mind how you go.

Pinocchio (*looking back*)   Don't worry about me.

He walks straight into a wall.

PINOCCHIO IS ASSAULTED AND DIES

Night-time. Outside.

Pinocchio *is alone and spooked.*

[Possible Narration: *As he walks through the night, the* **Actor playing Geppetto** *appears and narrates . . .*

Actor playing Geppetto   And so Pinocchio set off alone in the glooming dark, terrified for his very life, for the forest seemed to be alive.]

The moon, owls, birds, ghosts. **Pinocchio** *stumbles along whistling his tune (in a minor key) to keep his spirits up. A* **Bird** *scares* **Pinocchio**. *He leaps back.*

Pinocchio   Who goes there?

An echo, echo, echo, echo.

Pinocchio   Oh, no . . . (oh, no . . . oh, no . . . oh, no).

Pinocchio *is terrified. He creeps along (to creepy music) Then suddenly . . .*

Cricket   Evening!

Pinocchio   Who are you?

Cricket   Who do you think I am? I'm the ghost of the talking cricket.

Pinocchio   What are you doing here?

Cricket   I'm here to warn you to take your four gold coins and go back to Geppetto at once.

Pinocchio   But I'm going to the Field of Miracles.

Cricket   Don't trust anyone who promises easy riches. Go home or all will be lost.

Pinocchio   But I'm going to become a millionaire.

Cricket   You're going to be fleeced. Do as you're told and go home at once.

Pinocchio   Shut up, you stupid little insect.

Cricket   Mark my words.

Pinocchio   I'll squash you.

Pinocchio *wields a stick and tries to kill the* **Cricket** – *maybe he does / maybe it disappears and he is equally spooked.*

Pinocchio   What a life! All anyone ever wants to do is spoil things. If it's not Geppetto it's some stupid blackbird, if it's not the blackbird it's that self-righteous cricket. What's going to happen, eh? I suppose they think I'll run into a couple of murderers. Well, I'll tell you one thing. There aren't any murderers that are going to scare me.

During **Pinocchio**'s *speech the* **Cat** *and the* **Fox** *have been creeping up in disguise, as ghosts.*

Cat   Boo!

Pinocchio *screams and almost jumps out of his skin.*

Cat   Your money or your life.

Pinocchio   Aaaghgh!

Pinocchio *sticks the money in his mouth and keeps it firmly shut.*

Fox   Come on, give us your money.

Pinocchio *tries to say 'I haven't got any' but his mouth is full.*

Cat   What?

Pinocchio *tries again – just gurgling.*

Cat   If you don't hand over your money you're a dead man.

Fox   And after we kill you, we'll kill your father too.

Pinocchio   Oh, no not my father.

Pinocchio *realises he has revealed the gold coins to the robbers and clamps his jaw shut again.*

Cat   Now we've got you.

Fox   Open up.

Cat   Spit it out.

Pinoccchio *doesn't spit. They try to open his jaw but it is clamped shut. They use a knife, chisel, etc. to no avail. Then, in among this struggle,* **Pinocchio** *bites off the* **Cat**'s *paw, but clamps his mouth tightly shut. The* **Cat** *is in agony and the* **Fox** *is scared and flustered by the violence, so* **Pinocchio** *takes his chance and runs off.*

The Chase – **Pinocchio** *is more lithe and agile than either the* **Cat** *or the* **Fox***. They run around the stage / auditorium / change scale etc. The* **Cat** *and the* **Fox** *suffer great humiliations, but finally* **Pinocchio** *scampers up somewhere high where the* **Cat** *and the* **Fox** *are unable to get to him. By the time the* **Cat** *and the* **Fox** *get to him they are battered and worn by the arduous journey. They try to shout up but are out of breath. The* **Cat** *has a good idea and tries to explain it but because she is still out of breath she just gets on with it. They build a fire to smoke* **Pinocchio** *out.* **Pinocchio***, seeing the flames, leaps from his perch and runs off. The* **Cat** *and the* **Fox** *are disconsolate and reluctantly give chase.*
Pinocchio *reaches a house and bangs on the door.*

Pinocchio   Help! Help! Let me in.

A **Girl** *appears.*

Girl   Go away.

Pinocchio   Help! Help! I'm being chased by horrible assassins.

Girl   Go away. It's the middle of the night. And everybody here is dead.

Pinocchio   What about you? Couldn't you let me in?

Girl   But I'm dead too.

Pinocchio   Well, what are you doing at that window?

Girl   I'm waiting for the undertakers to take me away.

Pinocchio   Please, please, beautiful little girl with the blue hair, this is serious. I plead for your mercy.

The **Cat** *and the* **Fox** *arrive.*

Cat   Too late.

The **Cat** *and the* **Fox** *drag* **Pinocchio** *off, kicking and screaming. They brutally assault him. They take a drill to his mouth; it doesn't work.*

Fox   The wood's too hard.

They get all sorts of other implements in a macabre torture session. Each attempt to extract the money is to no avail. Finally . . .

Cat   I know. We'll hang him.

Fox   Brilliant. How?

The **Cat** *and the* **Fox** *hang* **Pinocchio***. There is lots of comic business where they bungle each step, tying themselves in knots. They abuse each other for their hopelessness: 'Bread brain', 'Squirrel-sniffer', 'Poo-handler', 'Skunk breath' etc. It all rises to a comic climax. But then they manage it.* **Pinocchio** *is hauled hideously into the air. The scene changes mood and becomes horrible.* **Pinocchio** *is in great distress. He is obviously choking. The* **Cat** *and the* **Fox** *wait for the money to fall, but nothing happens apart from* **Pinocchio** *choking to death.*

Cat   You may as well spit it out now. If you don't we'll just come back in the morning.

The **Cat** *and the* **Fox** *give up for the day and leave* **Pinocchio** *to die. The wind blows.* **Pinocchio** *is alone on stage, hanging.*

Hanging Song

> There's a full moon at my shoulder;
> There are stars around my eyes;
> There's a chill wind up my trousers
> And it's blowing up my thighs.
> And now my neck is hurting me
> And I think I'm fading fast,
> And I wish I'd gone to school now
> As this breath could be my last.
>
> But O what a beautiful world,
> O what a beautiful sky.
> So Papa please forgive me
> When I die,
> When I die.
>
> There are puddles in the darkness
> Filled with shiny little moons;
> They're singing little lullabies
> And some other sleepy tunes.
> And all my strength is fading fast,
> Please, please don't forsake me now,
> Cos I've never seen a circus
> And I've never milked a cow.
>
> O what a beautiful world.
> The birds have gone to bed.
> But Papa don't forget me
> When I'm dead,
> When I'm dead.
>
> O what a wonderful world
> Where so much has gone on,
> But I'll be doing nothing
> When I'm gone,
> When I'm . . .

As he sings the rope gets tighter and tighter, till finally he chokes and passes out. By the end of the song he slumps, presumably dead. A long pause to let this sink in.

INTERVAL

Act Two

The wind blows wilder. **Pinocchio**'s *body rocks in the gale. From her window the little* **Girl** *appears. She looks mournfully at* **Pinocchio**. *She claps her hands and a* **Bird** *appears. She claps her hands again and the* **Bird** *rescues* **Pinocchio**. *He is taken down from the tree and laid out in a bed in the little* **Girl**'s *house.*

PINOCCHIO IS BROUGHT BACK TO LIFE

The House of the Dead.

Solemn music accompanies the laying out of **Pinocchio**. *When the* **Bird** *has laid him out there is a sudden break of mood with a knock at the door and the three* **Doctors** *come in. The* **Doctors** *fuss and cluck around the corpse like the Marx Brothers or the Three Stooges. They listen with stethoscopes to his feet, the bang him with mallets, etc. They are no better than the* **Cat** *and the* **Fox**.

Owl   I've never seen anything like it in my life.

Raven   Most unusual.

Cricket   Very serious indeed.

Girl   But is he alive or dead?

Owl   I beg your pardon?

Girl   Is he alive or dead?

Raven   What sort of question is that?

Owl   Alive or dead?

Raven   Of course he's alive or dead.

They prod, poke and take his pulse. Tut gravely, etc.

Owl   Well, in my professional opinion, and I speak as someone with huge experience, he is absolutely and categorically dead. He is deceased, kaput, gone to another world, popped his clogs and gone to the sweet hereafter.

Unless, of course, he's alive, which would be a strong indication that he isn't dead at all.

Raven   An interesting hypothesis but one I think you will find is completely erroneous. For me, on the contrary, the puppet is alive and well, and if by some misfortune he is not alive and well, then, in fact, he is dead.

Girl   And what do you say?

Cricket   I haven't said anything. In my strict medical opinion I believe it is best to remain silent till proven otherwise.

Raven   Here, here.

Cricket   Besides, I am familiar with the creature, having in a previous life been a talking cricket and ethical adviser to the said reprobate, and can confirm his current state is entirely due to his predilection for laziness, greed, ignorance . . .

Pinocchio's *eyes open – he sees the* **Cricket** *and quickly closes them.*

Cricket   . . . sloth, rudeness, lack of discipline, frivolous enjoyment of sweets, plays etc., etc., etc. In short, he is a disgrace to puppetry and will cause his father to die of a broken heart.

Everybody is amazed at the **Cricket**'s *outburst. Then suddenly, in the hiatus, they hear a whimper. They all look at one another – then all look under the sheet.* **Pinocchio** *is crying.*

Raven   I don't want to panic anybody but this may be a sign that the patient has recovered.

Owl   On the contrary, I believe the puppet is merely crying because he is sad to have died.

Girl   Don't be so ridiculous. You're supposed to be doctors. Get out of here at once.

Owl   I beg your pardon?

Girl   Get out. All of you.

Raven   You will be hearing from my lawyer.

Owl   You will be hearing from my accountant.

Cricket   You will be hearing from my chiropodist.

Girl   Get out!

The little **Girl** *runs over to* **Pinocchio** *with a white powder dissolved in some water. She tends to him and plays the role of a nurse / mother.*

Girl   Now, come, take this medicine and in a few days you will be better.

Pinocchio *looks at it with a pained expression.*

Pinocchio   What's it taste like?

Girl   It tastes fine. Now drink it down like a good boy.

Pinocchio   But is it bitter or sweet?

Girl   It's a little bit bitter but it'll do you good.

Pinocchio   I'm not drinking it if it's bitter.

Girl   Look, drink it. It will do you good.

Pinocchio   I don't like anything bitter.

Girl   OK. Drink it, and after you've drunk it I'll give you a lump of sugar to take away the taste.

Pinocchio   Where's the lump of sugar?

Girl   Here it is. Now, drink the drink.

Pinocchio   Can't I have the sugar first and then I'll drink the drink?

Girl   If you promise to drink the drink.

Pinocchio   I promise.

Girl   OK.

*The **Girl** gives him the sugar and he devours it, licking his lips.*

Pinocchio   Mm. I wish sugar were medicine.

Girl   Now keep your promise and drink your few drops of water, and you'll get well again.

Pinocchio (*taking the glass and sticking his nose in it*)   It's too bitter. I can't drink it.

Girl   How do you know? You haven't even tasted it.

Pinocchio   You can tell. I've smelt it. I want another lump of sugar and then I'll drink it.

Girl   Look, here's another lump of sugar. Now, drink it or you'll never get well.

Pinocchio *eats the sugar, then raises the glass to his lips.*

Pinocchio   I can't do it.

Girl   Why not?

Pinocchio   The cushion's not right.

*The **Girl** takes the cushion away.*

Pinocchio   It's no use.

Girl   What now?

Pinocchio   The door is ajar.

*The **Girl** closes the door.*

Girl   There.

Pinocchio   Anyway, I thought you were dead.

Girl   Drink.

Pinocchio   I can't.

Girl   You'll be sorry.

Pinocchio   I don't care.

Girl   If you don't drink it you'll be off to the next world in half an hour.

Pinocchio   I don't care. I'd rather die than taste this hideous medicine.

Girl   Right!

Either the little **Girl** *forces it on him and he leaps up as right as rain to avoid having to take it, or:*

There is a bang. The door flies open and the hideous figure of the **Rabbit of Death** *enters. He marches round the room in a funereal manner.* **Pinocchio** *is terrified. He quakes.*

Pinocchio   Who are you?

Rabbit of Death   I am the Rabbit of Death and I will take you to hell if you don't drink your medicine.

Pinocchio *picks up the medicine and drinks it down in one.*

Rabbit of Death   Another wasted journey.

The **Rabbit of Death** *leaves.*

PINOCCHIO LIES AND HIS NOSE GROWS

Pinocchio *feels better and jumps up.*

Pinocchio   See? I feel better already.

Girl   Anyway, how come you were dead in the first place?

Pinocchio   It wasn't my fault. First I was born, then I stole my father's wig, then I ran away, then I came back, then I burnt my feet, then I went to school, then I saw the theatre, then I went to the Field of Miracles, then there were these ghosts who came for my gold coins and then I was hanged and then it's now.

Girl   And where are your gold coins?

Pinocchio   I lost them.

His nose grows.

Girl   Really? Where did you lose them?

Pinocchio   Oh . . . erm . . . well . . . erm. I lost them in the forest late at night, when it was completely dark and you couldn't see anything.

His nose grows more.

Girl   Well, we haven't got any time to waste. Come on, we'd better look for them.

Pinocchio   Wait . . . erm . . . oh, I've just remembered that I didn't lose them at all but a terrible thing happened to them and I swallowed them when I was drinking the medicine.

His nose grows to an incredible length.

Lazzo of the nose getting in the way. **Pinocchio** *is in a terrible state. The* **Girl** *laughs at him.*

Pinocchio   Help me! Do something.

Girl   Hahaha.

Pinocchio   What are you laughing at?

Girl   You and your lies.

Pinocchio   What lies?

Girl   Your long-nosed lies.

Pinocchio *is running around trying to hide his nose. He bumps into things and is getting more and more frantic.*

Girl   That'll teach you.

Pinocchio   I'm sorry. I'm sorry.

Girl   Are you really sorry?

Pinocchio   Yes, I am really completely and utterly sorry.

Girl   OK. I'll get some woodpeckers to come and chop it down to size for you.

Pinocchio   What!

The **Girl** *claps and a swarm of* **Woodpeckers** *appear and chop his nose down to size.* **Pinocchio** *screams in agony. The* **Woodpeckers** *disappear and the* **Girl** *sticks a plaster on the end of his nose and kisses it better.*

Pinocchio   Oh, thank you, thank you, little dead girl.

Girl   I'm not the little dead girl any more. I'm a fairy.

Pinocchio   Oh, I love you, little fairy.

Girl   I love you too. Will you stay with me and be my brother? And I'll be your good little sister too.

Pinocchio   I would love to stay, but what about my poor father?

Girl   But you can stay here. I've thought of everything and I've told a little bird to tell your father and he's coming right here. He'll be here before nightfall.

Pinocchio *jumps for joy.*

Pinocchio   Yippee! Well, I must go and greet him. If that's all right with you, I will go and kiss my poor old dad who has suffered so much in this world because of me.

Girl   All right, but watch how you go. Take the forest path and you'll be sure to meet him soon.

Pinocchio *jumps around excitedly.*

Pinocchio   'Bye!

Girl   See you later.

Pinocchio   'Bye!

The **Girl** *looks on sadly as* **Pinocchio** *runs off.*

PINOCCHIO GOES OFF TO MEET HIS FATHER BUT IS DIVERTED

Pinocchio *walks along, singing, 'I'm going to see my dad, I'm going to see my dad.' He walks across and then off stage. Then* **Geppetto** *comes on and goes off just as* **Pinocchio** *comes on from another* *direction. They criss-cross like this for some time, using all the old gags where two people just miss each other. Finally, they both head off in different directions then . . . .*

Change of scene.

The **Cat** *and the* **Fox**, *looking at the empty tree.*

Cat   I don't understand. How could he have got down?

Fox   He got down because you are a complete blithering moron. I thought you knew how to tie knots.

Cat   Maybe there's something we don't know. Maybe he's some kind of monster.

Fox   He's just a stupid puppet. If you weren't such a klutz we'd have the money by now.

Cat   Look at my hand. That's all your fault.

Fox   Let it teach you a lesson.

The **Fox** *hits the* **Cat** *around the head.*

Fox   I should've strung you up there. I don't have to put up with this amateur behaviour, you know. I was quite respectable in my day.

Cat   What on earth are we going to do now?

Enter **Pinocchio**.

Pinocchio   Hello.

Fox (*absent-mindedly*)   Hello.

They suddenly realise who it is.

Fox   Ah, Mr Pinocchio.

Cat   How great it is to see you. I mean, to hear your squeaky little voice.

Fox   A singular pleasure, if ever there was one. But Mr Pinocchio, what happened? When we came back to the inn after our little emergency, it seemed you had disappeared.

Cat   I hope we didn't offend you in some way.

Pinocchio   No, not at all. I only wish you had've been with me. Something terrible happened.

Cat   No!

Pinocchio   I was attacked.

Cat *and* **Fox**   Attacked!

Pinocchio   By assassins!

Cat *and* **Fox**   Assassins!

Pinocchio   Then I ran and then they ran after me and I saw this bush and I jumped over and they jumped over and then I came to a hedge and . . .

Fox   OK, OK, get to the point.

Pinocchio   Then I was horribly hanged from the Great Oak Tree.

Fox   Oh, my goodness.

Cat   What a terrible, terrible business!

Fox   What a sad and dangerous world we honest men are condemned to live in.

Pinocchio *notices the* **Cat**'s *wounded paw.*

Pinocchio   Are you all right?

Cat   Oh, it's nothing.

Pinocchio   But you've lost your paw, Ms Cat.

Cat   No, I haven't.

Fox   She lent it to someone.

Pinocchio   Lent it to someone?

Fox   That's right, a wolf.

Cat   Yes, we came across a wolf, starving on the road, and out of the kindness of my heart I bit it off and gave it to him to stave off his hunger.

Fox (*almost in tears*)   A most noble act, if you don't mind me saying so.

Pinocchio   Oh, what a wonderful world for mice it would be if all cats were like you.

Cat   And what are you doing here so bright and early?

Pinocchio   I'm going to meet my father to give him the gold coins.

Fox   Sorry, which coins were those?

Cat   The ones that . . .

The **Fox** *has to physically shut the* **Cat** *up.*

Pinocchio   Remember the ones that I was going to bury in the Field of Miracles.

Fox   Of course we remember. What a great pity you didn't make it.

Cat   What a rich man you could be.

Pinocchio   Puppet.

Cat   Sorry, puppet.

Fox   Listen, I've got a wonderful idea. Why don't we go there now?

Cat   Where?

Pinocchio   Where?

Fox   The Field of Miracles.

Pinocchio   But I've got to meet my father and go back to the little fairy girl's house.

Fox   But if we went there quickly we'd be back in no time.

Pinocchio   But I thought you had to plant them overnight.

Fox   Ah, but today is the special day where you only need twenty minutes.

Cat   Is it?

Fox (*aside*)   Of course it is, you dimwit.

Pinocchio (*thinking*)   No. It's all right. I'll go another day. Maybe tomorrow.

Fox (*damning* **Pinocchio**)   Shoot.

Cat   But didn't you hear? Tomorrow the Field of Miracles is being bought by a rich man and privatised.

Pinocchio   Really?

Cat   Oh, yes. I'd go there at once if I were you.

Pinocchio   Is it really the last day for the Field of Miracles.

Cat   Well, actually, I just . . .

Fox   Yes. It's completely the very last day.

Cat   It's the very last minutes of the very last day.

Pinocchio (*thinks for some time*)   Are you sure?

Cat   Of course he's sure

Pinocchio   Well, it would be a terrible thing to disappoint my poor Papa.

Fox   Of course it would

Pinocchio   And it'll only take twenty minutes?

Cat   Look, come on.

They go off to The Field of Miracles.

THE FIELD OF MIRACLES

The scene changes to a bleak landscape. The **Cat** *and the* **Fox** *and* **Pinocchio** *come on again, exhausted, as if they'd been a thousand miles.*

Fox   Here we are.

Pinocchio   This is it?

Cat   Can't you feel the magic?

Pinocchio   What do I do?

Fox   Take your money.

Cat   Dig a little hole.

Fox   Pop it in the ground.

Cat   Bury it.

Fox   Pat it down.

Cat   Say the magic word.

Pinocchio   What magic word?

Cat   I don't know. Abracadabra.

Fox   And then leave it for twenty minutes.

Pinocchio   Can't I watch?

Fox   No, of course you can't watch.

Pinocchio   Why not?

Cat   Because it won't bloody well work, will it.

Fox   You have to walk twenty paces.

Pinocchio *walks twenty paces.*

Pinocchio   1, 2, 3, 4, 5, 6, 7, 8, 9, 10, 11, 12, 13, 14, 15, 6, 17, 18, 19, 20.

Pinocchio *walks off stage.*

Fox (*calling*)   Now close your eyes.

Cat (*calling*)　Then count to twenty thousand.

Pinocchio (*off stage*)　I don't know how to count to twenty thousand.

Fox　Just keep counting up to three until we tell you.

Cat　And don't open your eyes.

The **Cat** *and the* **Fox** *make off with the money.*

Pinocchio (*still off*)　OK. 1, 2, 3, 1, 2, 3, 1, 2, 3, 1, 2, 3, 1, 2, 3, 1, 2, 3, 1, 2, 3, twenty thousand. It must be twenty thousand by now. How rich I am going to be . . . (*He comes on.*) . . . with a library of almond cakes and a cellar full of whipped cream . . . (*He sees there is nothing. His face looks panicked.*) But . . . where is the sovereign tree? (*He runs to the earth.*) Where's it gone? Somebody's stolen it. Somebody's stolen my fortune.

He starts to dig desperately in the ground. He digs further and further down. More and more hysterically. A **Bird** *up above laughs and laughs.* **Pinocchio** *finds something in the earth. He gasps.*

Pinocchio　What's this?

Pinocchio *brushes the earth off a tombstone.*

Bird　It's a tombstone, stupid.

Pinocchio　Why is it a tombstone?

Bird　Because somebody's dead.

Pinocchio　Who? Who's dead?

Bird　Read it.

Pinocchio　I can't. I've never been to school.

Bird　I'll read it. 'Here lies the little girl with blue hair who died of grief for having been abandoned by her little brother Pinocchio.'

Pinocchio　That's me.

Bird　I know.

Pinocchio   But does that mean I killed the little girl with blue hair?

Bird   'Fraid so.

Pinocchio   You mean she's dead? Again?

Pinocchio *takes this in. He gets very upset.*

Pinocchio   But this is terrible. Why couldn't I have died instead of her? How come I killed her? She was my only little friend who saved my life.

He breaks down. **Pinocchio** *beats on the grave.*

Pinocchio   Please come back to life. Please come back to life and tell me where my father is. Oh, I wish someone would come and make a table out of my legs. I wish the assassins would come and bash me on the head and use my arms for firewood.

Bird   Steady on, guv'nor.

Pinocchio   Go away, you meddling bird.

Bird   But . . .

Pinocchio   I'm sick of talking animals.

Bird   All I was going to say was I know where your father is.

Pinocchio *is boo-hooing and takes no notice of anything the* **Bird** *is saying. Then he suddenly stops crying altogether.*

Pinocchio   What!!??

Bird   I saw him down by the seaside. He was looking for you when you didn't show up at the fairy house.

Pinocchio   So he's not dead after all. Yippee!

Bird   Look, come on. I'll take you.

THE FLIGHT TO THE SEA

Pinocchio *gets on the* **Bird***'s back and they soar over the countryside. Lazzo of the* **Bird** *in flight.*

They arrive at the sea.

Pinocchio   I don't see him anywhere. Where is my poor father?

Bird   Look. There he is!

Pinocchio   Where?

Bird   There in a boat?

Pinocchio   What is he doing in boat?

Bird   Looking for you, of course.

Pinocchio   Daddy! Daddy!

The sea is getting rougher.

Pinocchio   He can't hear me. Look, Daddy. It's me Pinocchio! Flying on a magic bird!

Suddenly, the little **Geppetto** *puppet hears* **Pinocchio**.

Pinocchio   Pinocchio! Pinoccchio!

Just as we think things will be all right, suddenly there is a huge wave which knocks the boat (pan) into the air.

Geppetto   Aaaaagghhhh!

Pinocchio   Oh, Daddy!

Geppetto *flies through the air and the wave covers him.*

Pinocchio *looks down.* **Geppetto** *and the pan have disappeared.*

Pinocchio   He's gone.

Pinocchio *waits.* **Geppetto** *does not reappear. He waits. Nothing.*

Pinocchio   Did you see? My father has drowned. Don't worry. I'll save you

Bird   No! No, Pinocchio.

Pinocchio *takes no notice and jumps down in slow motion.*

Bird   No! No! The sea will retreat and you'll fall on the . . .

The sea retreats and he lands on . . .

Bird   . . . the land.

Pinocchio *falls onto the land.*

Stunned silence. It must seem like **Pinocchio** *is dead. He doesn't move.*

The stage clears and **Pinocchio** *is left all alone. The little* **Girl** *appears brushing blue feathers off her shoulders. She looks at the prone* **Pinocchio** *sadly. After a beat,* **Pinocchio** *looks up.*

Pinocchio   I thought you were dead.

Girl   I could say the same about you.

Pinocchio   Where am I? Where's my father? Is he dead?

Girl   I wouldn't be surprised if he was with a naughty son like you. I thought I told you to be good and go straight to him. Listen, if you don't go to school and be a good little boy we'll all end up in a mess.

Pinocchio   Please, tell me he isn't dead.

Girl   I can't tell you anything. All I can do is to tell you to go to school and learn to be a sensible little puppet or this will just be the start of your sorrows.

Pinocchio   I don't want to go to school. I want my Daddy.

Girl   Look, you stupid puppet. You're an orphan now. If you don't start growing up and being responsible you're going to end up in all sorts of trouble. And If you go to school. I'll give you a kiss.

Pinocchio   Promise?

Girl   Promise.

Pinocchio *goes to receive his kiss.*

Girl   After you've been to school.

Pinocchio   Before.

Girl   After.

Pinocchio   Before.

Girl   Oh, OK then. But you have to promise.

Pinocchio   I promise.

The **Girl** *'magics' on the schoolroom.*

Pinocchio   I'm going to be the best student in the whole wide world. You'll see.

Girl   I'm counting on you, Pinocchio.

Pinocchio *skips off to school.*

SCHOOL

School bell. A class forms – they are absolutely unruly. Things fly, noise. Fights. **Pinocchio** *comes in as good as gold.*

Boy   Ooooooooooooo!

Pinocchio   Hello.

Boy *gestures towards a seat for* **Pinocchio** *to sit down.*

Pinocchio   Thank you.

The **Boy** *pulls the seat away from* **Pinocchio** *and he falls. Everyone laughs.*

Boy   Terribly sorry.

Pinocchio   It's quite all right.

Pinocchio *goes to sit down. This time the same thing happens or a pin is put on the seat. After much fooling around at* **Pinocchio**'s *expense he manages to sit down. He prepares for the lesson.*

Boy   Pst. You can't wear your cap in here.

Pinocchio *takes it off. The* **Boys** *put something horrible on his head, then steal his hat.* **Pinocchio** *runs around, trying to retrieve it.*

Pinocchio   Give me that back. My father made that.

Finally, after much baiting, he gets it back. Basically, this whole section is a lazzo of dirty tricks. (They tie a string to his nose, kick him up the backside when he bends down to pick up his book etc.)

Pinocchio   Why are you being like this? All I want is to be a proper boy.

Lampwick   Christ, you sound like little Miss Muffet.

Pinocchio   Who?

Lampwick *gets a spider and puts it down* **Pinocchio**'*s shirt.* **Pinocchio** *freaks out. When he has got rid of the spider he grabs* **Lampwick**. *No one was prepared for this. He has* **Lampwick** *by the throat when the teacher comes in.*

Teacher   What on earth is going on here? Who are you?

Pinocchio   I'm Pinocchio.

Teacher   Well, I'm not having you coming here abusing our boys.

Pinocchio *gets a clip round the lughole.*

Teacher   Now, I'm having no more of this nonsense whatsoever. Sit down there.

Pinocchio *sits down. The register is taken.* '**Lampwick**', '*Lorenzo*', '*Dion*', '*Giuseppe*', *etc. During this time the boys taunt* **Pinocchio** *but he ignores them. Every time the* **Teacher** *looks up the boys are perfectly behaved; when he looks away they are horrible to* **Pinocchio**. *The* **Teacher** *reads out a very long list of boys who are 'not here, sir'.*

Finally, a **Boy** *kicks* **Pinocchio**. **Pinocchio** *can stand no more. He kicks the boy back. It nearly cripples the boy.*

Boy   Aaaaaaggghhhh.

Teacher   What's this?

Boy   He kicked me, sir.

Teacher   What is the meaning of this? I've warned you.

Pinocchio   But . . .

Teacher   Come here.

Pinocchio *goes out front. He is made to hold out his hand. The* **Teacher** *wields the ruler. Lazzo of avoiding the ruler.* **Pinocchio** *eventually gets hit and goes back to his chair.*

Lampwick (*next to* **Pinocchio**)   Hey, nice kick. You nearly broke his leg.

Pinocchio   I didn't mean to hurt him, really.

Lampwick   It was cool. I've been trying to get that idiot for weeks now.

Teacher   Right. Now we are going to do the alphabet.

The **Boys** *groan and make faces as the* **Teacher** *sets up the ABC chart. The* **Teacher** *points to each letter.*

Teacher   Right. A. A is for . . . ?

Silence.

Teacher   A is for . . . ?

Lampwick   Arse.

Everybody *laughs.*

Teacher   Who said that?

Everybody   Pinocchio.

Pinocchio   Sir, I didn't. Honest.

Teacher   I will not tolerate that sort of language in my class. I'll ask you again. What is A for?

Pinocchio *thinks.*

Pinocchio   An elephant.

Teacher   Don't be so ridiculous. Sit down.

The **Teacher** *turns back to the chart.*

Teacher   A is for anabasis, articulation or arithmetic. B. B
is for . . . ?

Boy   Bottom!

The **Teacher** *spins round.*

Pinocchio   Sir, it wasn't me.

Teacher   All right, what is B for?

Pinocchio *thinks.*

Pinocchio   Balls.

Everyone *laughs.*

Teacher   That's it.

The **Teacher** *hits* **Pinocchio**.

Pinocchio   What's wrong with balls?

Everybody *laughs at* **Pinocchio** *getting hit.*

Teacher   Right, that's it. If everyone is going to
encourage such puerile behaviour, one hundred lines for
everyone: 'I must not be childish in class.' In silence.

The **Boys** *have to do their lines reluctantly.*

Boy 1   This is your fault.

Boy 2   We're going to get you.

Teacher   In silence, I said.

Lampwick (*of the* **Teacher**)   What a tosspot. Listen, do
you fancy bunking off at break time?

Pinocchio   I beg your pardon?

Lampwick   D'ya fancy going down to the beach? I heard
there's a whale going to land.

Pinocchio   A whale! Wow.

Lampwick   Well, come and see it. It only takes half an hour.

Pinocchio   But what about school?

Lampwick   What about school? It stinks.

Pinocchio   Well, I suppose a whale is quite educational. But can't we go after school?

Lampwick   Don't be so stupid, you block of balsa. The whale isn't going to stick around till home time.

Pinocchio   But what will sir say?

Lampwick   Who cares what sir says? He's paid to stand around moaning. It'll probably make his day.

Pinocchio   But what about my poor mum?

Lampwick   For crying out loud, don't tell your mum.

Pinocchio   What? Oh, I see. Brilliant. Brilliant idea.

Teacher   You two. What have you been doing? You haven't even written a single line. Right. Out front. Trousers down.

Pinocchio   I beg your pardon?

Teacher   Trousers down.

Pinocchio *reluctantly bends over. The* **Teacher** *picks up a huge ruler and steps back to get a real good run in. Just as he prepares to deal* **Pinocchio** *a horrid blow, the bell rings and* **Pinocchio** *zooms out of the door as if it were a starting gun for a race. The kids cheer and they all run out with him. They run round and round, and head for the beach.* **Pinocchio** *heads the pack of screaming kids. It's like* Lord of the Flies. *Finally, they reach the beach.*

PINOCCHIO GETS IN A FIGHT AND A BOY GETS KILLED

Pinocchio   Where's the whale?

Lampwick   You didn't really think there was going to be a whale, did you?

Pinocchio   But you made me miss school.

Lampwick   But it's a good thing. Aren't you ashamed of working hard?

Pinocchio   I thought it was good to work hard.

Lampwick   That's the most selfish thing I've heard.

Pinocchio   Selfish?

Lampwick   Well, if you work hard, you make everyone else look stupid.

Pinocchio   I don't make anyone look stupid.

Boy   Yes, you do. (*He pushes* **Pinocchio**.) Swot.

Pinocchio   Jackass.

It quickly escalates into a fight. The **Boy** *hits* **Pinocchio**. **Pinocchio** *hits him back.* **Pinocchio**'s *wooden feet and hands are vicious weapons and he is impervious to pain. Soon a mass battle has broken out. Perhaps* **Lampwick** *takes* **Pinocchio**'s *side. Books fly everywhere.*

In the middle the **Cricket** *appears.*

Cricket   Stop all this, you good-for-nothing rascals.

Pinocchio   Oh, shut up, you tedious flea.

The **Cricket** *is squashed. A* **Boy** *picks up* **Pinocchio**'s *book and aims a mighty blow at* **Pinocchio**'s *head.* **Pinocchio** *ducks and the full impact lands on another* **Boy**'s *head. The* **Boy** *falls to the ground, badly injured. Suddenly, the hilarious, balletic fight has become gravely serious. Everybody runs away, leaving* **Pinocchio** *to tend the* *dying child. The* **Boy** *moans.* **Pinocchio** *rests his head, then runs around in panic.*

Pinocchio   Please don't die. Please don't die.

He runs to the sea and bathes his handkerchief in the water to soothe the **Boy***'s head.*

Pinocchio   Please, please don't die. I'll go to school. I'll do anything you like. Please.

Pinocchio *does everything he can to save the* **Boy***. Artificial respiration etc.*

Pinocchio   Please don't die. I'll never be able to face my poor mammy again.

The **Boy** *dies in* **Pinocchio***'s arms.* **Pinocchio** *is horrified. He kisses him. Crying,* **Pinocchio** *holds the body in lonely desperation.*

Pinocchio   What's become of me? What's become of me?

A **Carabiniere** *arrives.*

Carabiniere   Hello, hello, hello. What's all this, then?

Pinocchio   Please, my poor friend is ill.

Carabiniere   Ill? This lad is dead as a dodo. Who did this?

Pinocchio   I don't know, sir.

Carabiniere   He's been hit on the head by this book.

Pinocchio   Has he?

Carabiniere   Well, whose book is it?

Pinocchio   Mine, sir.

Carabiniere   Right. You're coming along with me, son.

Pinocchio   But I . . .

Carabiniere   On your feet, you murdering scoundrel.

Pinocchio   But I didn't do anything. I'm completely innocent.

Carabiniere   A likely story. Going around with dangerous literature. They'll bang you away for a very long time, son.

Pinocchio   Please, this is all a big mistake.

Carabiniere   Listen, there's no mistake, son.

The **Carabiniere** *frogmarches* **Pinocchio** *along the beach.* **Pinocchio** *runs off. The* **Carabiniere** *is about to give chase when the dead boy wakes up and moans. The* **Carabiniere** *is distracted.* **Lampwick** *appears from the trapdoor and whistles to* **Pinocchio**. **Pinocchio**, *seeing the* **Carabiniere** *isn't paying attention, takes his chance and jumps down the hole. As the* **Carabiniere** *looks back to* **Pinocchio**, *he sees he has disappeared and goes off grumpily. He kicks the* **Boy** *on the ground.*

Carabiniere   And get to school, you little layabout.

He leaves, as does the dazed **Boy**.

LAMPWICK ENTICES PINOCCHIO TO PLAYLAND

Lampwick *and* **Pinocchio** *come out of the trapdoor.*

Lampwick   That was lucky.

Pinocchio   I thought I was going to get thrown in jail.

Lampwick   Don't worry, that old windbag couldn't catch a cold. Here.

Lampwick *gives* **Pinocchio** *a pipe.*

Pinocchio   What is it?

Lampwick   It's good for you. It's what real men do.

Pinocchio   Brilliant.

Lazzo of lighting the pipe. **Lampwick** *finds smoking makes him a bit queasy but masks it.* **Pinocchio** *almost lights the wrong end. He* *smokes – it makes him feel sick, he coughs, gets woozy, smokes too much, falls over. Then smokes like a pro.*

Pinocchio   Well, we'd better be getting back to school, then.

Lampwick   You're not really serious, are you?

Pinocchio   But we have to go to school sometimes.

Lampwick   No you don't. Only if you want to turn into one of them.

Pinocchio   'Them'?

Lampwick   If you've got any sense at all you should run away with me.

Pinocchio   Where are you going?

Lampwick   Where am I going? Only the greatest place in the entire universe.

Pinocchio   Where's that, then?

Lampwick   You mean you don't know?

Pinocchio   No.

Lampwick   Playland.

Pinocchio   Playland?

Lampwick   Come.

Pinocchio   Certainly not. I've got to see my mum, who's really a fairy, and be well-behaved and get turned into a proper boy.

Lampwick   You mean you'd rather be well-behaved with your old mum than be in Playland where there are no schools and no teachers or books or anything? Where the summer holidays start on January first and don't end till the last day in December?

Pinocchio   And what do they do in Playland?

Lampwick   Whatever they like. During the day you play all day and have loads of fun, and in the night you go to sleep, and the next day you get up and play all day again.

Pinocchio   That's what I call civilisation.

Lampwick   So you're coming? The wagon'll be here soon.

Pinocchio   But I can't. I promised the fairy to be a good puppet.

Lampwick   You're not coming because you 'promised a fairy'?

Pinocchio   Have a lovely time. 'Bye.

Lampwick   Where are you going?

Pinocchio   I've got to be back before dark.

Lampwick   Just wait two minutes.

Pinocchio   But the fairy . . .

Lampwick   Look, Pinocchio, forget the fairy. Just let her yell if she yells. This is the last time you'll ever see me, Pinocchio.

Pinocchio   So, are you going on your own?

Lampwick   Are you kidding? There's hundreds of us.

Pinocchio   Wow! I wish the wagon were coming right now.

Lampwick   Why?

Pinocchio   So I could see you all off.

Lampwick   Well, just wait, then.

Pinocchio   No, I'd better go.

Pinocchio *hugs* **Lampwick** *and starts to leave.*

Pinocchio   And there are really no schools in Playland?

Lampwick   Nope. It's banned even to mention them.

Pinocchio   And you can play all day?

Lampwick   How many times do I have to go through it?

Pinocchio   Well, have a great time, then. (*He turns to leave, then looks back.*) And it's summer holidays every day of the year?

Lampwick *nods.*

Pinocchio   Maybe I'll just wait and see you off, then.

Lampwick   What about the fairy?

Pinocchio   Stuff the fairy.

The sound of the carriage.

Lampwick   Listen, here it comes.

On comes the wagon driven by a **Man** *and pulled by donkeys with men's shoes on.*

Man   Hello, little boys! All aboard for Playland!

The wagon is piled high with children.

Lampwick   Well, goodbye, then.

Lampwick *climbs up.*

Man   Are you sure you don't want to come too, my handsome little lad?

Pinocchio (*torn*)   No. I want to stay here and be a good puppet and stay at home and work and everything.

Man   Are you sure about that, my love?

Pinocchio *shakes his head.*

Pinocchio   No, no, no, no, no. Oh, go on, then.

Lampwick   Come on up.

Man   I'm afraid we're completely full up. You'll have to ride on the back of a donkey.

Pinocchio *tries to mount a donkey, but it kicks him off. The* **Man** *rushes over and bites the donkey's ear to chastise it.*

Man   Get back on, my lovely.

Pinocchio *gets on the donkey.*

Donkey   You idiot. Don't go there. You'll regret it.

Pinocchio *is shocked that the* **Donkey** *can talk. The* **Man** *cracks his whip.*

Donkey   Get off. It's your only chance.

Man   Off we go to Playland!

Pinocchio *looks down at the* **Donkey**; *he sees it is crying.*

Pinocchio   Wait, Mr Man. This donkey is crying.

Man   I'll skin that old mule before too long. No, there's no time to be wasted. There is play to be played.

The **Man** *sounds his horn or cracks his whip and they're off. The* **Boys** *scream with delight, shouting: 'Playland!'* **Pinocchio** *has to hold on tight, because off they go.*

PLAYLAND

Playland Song
 Where can children play all day?
 Where can we get our own way?
 Where can we do as we may?
 In Playland, Playland, Playland.
 Where can you get free pork pies?
 Where can children all tell lies?
 Where nobody believes their eyes,
 In Playland, Playland, Playland.

Chorus

 Playland – you can fire guns at dogs.
 Playland – you can dance about in clogs.
 Playland – you can write your name in bogs.
 Playland, Playland, Playland.

Where can children eat their fill
And never have to pay the bill,
And order pies until they're ill?
In Playland, Playland, Playland.
Where can children beat up wimps,
Trip up nits and fart on blimps,
And kick the teacher till he limps?
In Playland, Playland, Playland.

Chorus

Playland – you can play the big trombone.
Playland – you can stand there on your own.
Playland – you will never need to moan.
Playland, Playland, Playland.

Signs say 'Down wif Skool', 'Hurray for Fun and Gamz' etc.
The whole charabanc arrives in Playland. All the boys pile off. Circus
music. They immediately go into their wild play mode. Piggyback races.
Throwing stones into the audience. Dressing up. Rolling hoops, fun-
fights, imitating chickens, smoking cigarettes, singing songs and
behaving like adults.
*Each **Boy** finds hilarity in everyone else. It soon descends into*
*pandemonium. The **Man** is smiling and orchestrating all the games,*
and cries of 'Playland' elicit an echo of 'Playland' in response. There
are loads of fun things to do and funny wigs to wear. There is hilarity
*to the point of exhaustion. Eventually the **Boys** all fall asleep. They*
*huddle together like a load of drunks, **Pinocchio** bedding down with*
***Lampwick**, their arms around each other. They snooze like babies.*
*Soon the **Man** appears and wakes them all up rudely with a bell.*

Man   Playland!

They all leap up.

Man   Today we are going to play . . . Dancing!

*A sleepy but enthusiastic 'Hooray' from the **Boys**.*

Lampwick   Come on, Pinocchio

Pinocchio *gets up. Thunderous music starts and the* **Boys** *enjoy their outrageous dances – twists, sticking their bottoms out. A parody of every imaginable dance step. Sometimes in unison as a number, other times as organised chaos. Everybody is happy. Maybe they pass round a bottle of booze and they get drunk?*

Man   And now for the fabulous game of 'smashing up the school room'.

All the **Boys** *run out enthusiastically. We hear sounds of smashing off stage. They come back exhausted.*

Pinocchio   This is the best place I've ever been.

Lampwick   See? I told you.

Pinocchio   It's a bit tiring, though.

Lampwick   That's all right, it's Playland. Just have a snooze.

Pinocchio *and* **Lampwick** *settle down again. They have just got to sleep when the* **Man** *appears. He blows his horn. They sit up, startled. The* **Man** *smiles horribly.*

Man   Playland.

Pinocchio (*half-heartedly*)   Playland.

Man   Today is the day for . . .

Great expectation.

Man   More dancing!!

Boys   Hooray.

Man   Come on, you two.

Pinocchio *is feeling a bit the worse for wear now, but joins in the dancing. Each dancer shows off a ridiculous thing that the others find funny. Their dances are clearly* not *funny but just displays of indulgence. They all laugh hysterically at one another. If the audience laugh this time they laugh at* the **Boys** not *with them. Finally the music stops.* **Pinocchio** *and* **Lampwick** *are still laughing at one another.*

Pinocchio   This is the best life ever.

Lampwick   What did I tell you? And to think you wanted to stay in boring old normal land. If it were up to you you'd be doing your homework with your fairy.

Pinocchio   Hohoho.

Lampwick   Aren't you glad you came?

Pinocchio   Lampwick, I'm the luckiest puppet in the whole world to have a friend like you. You are the best friend in the whole wide world.

Lampwick   No, you're the best friend in the whole wide world.

Pinocchio   No, you're the best friend in the whole wide world.

They laugh and laugh.

Pinocchio   I think you're fantastic.

PINOCCHIO AND LAMPWICK TURN INTO
DONKEYS

They embrace and then start some affectionate horseplay. They laugh and laugh at their game. Gradually their laughing becomes a 'hee-haw'. Then they begin to adopt donkey mannerisms. They both get hysterics watching each other start to do that. This only seems to hasten their metamorphosis. Very soon they are hee-hawing and going down on all fours. Perhaps ears and tails appear. Both **Pinocchio** *and* **Lampwick** *laugh at each other and try to pretend that they are not turning into donkeys at all and, as a matter of fact, everything is fine.*

Lampwick   Are you all right?

Pinocchio   Fine. There's nothing wrong with me. Are you all right?

Lampwick   Never been better.

The more they deny that nothing is happening, the more donkey-like characteristics they assume, therefore the more they need to hide it. The cycle gets worse and worse, till it really isn't a joke any more.

Pinocchio   I think I'm turning into a heee-hawww.

Lampwick   What did you hee-haw?

They start to panic and get upset. The **Man** *appears.*

Pinocchio   What's happening to hee-haw?

Man   What do you mean?

Pinocchio   Look, we've grown hee-haw!

Man   It looks like you've come down with something. Don't worry, it's quite common.

Lampwick   What do you mean, it's quite common?

Man   Jackass fever. It happens to all the boys.

Pinocchio   Jackass hee-haw?

Man   Don't worry about it, it doesn't last long. Another ten minutes and you'll have changed into a mule for good.

The **Man** *laughs in a sinister manner. The* **Donkeys** *panic. The* **Man** *cracks a whip. He rounds up* **Lampwick** *with a few lashes to his backside.*

Lampwick   But I don't want to be a hee-haw!

Man   Too late. You're going to the coal mines, sonny. And if you don't shape up, you'll be going off to the knacker's yard, matey.

Lampwick   Hee-haw!

Man   How'd'ya think I keep this place running? I've made my fortune in glue.

Lampwick *is whipped off stage.* **Pinocchio** *is cowering in the corner. The* **Man** *comes back in.*

Man   It's all right, nobody's going to harm you. Have some straw.

Pinocchio   Hee-haw.

The **Man** *throws down some straw.*

Pinocchio   I can't eat hee-haw.

Man   What did you expect, chicken breast in aspic?

He whips **Pinocchio**.

Man   Get it eaten.

Pinocchio *eats the straw. Lazzo of eating the straw. It is horrible.*

Man   All right, all right. What do you think this is a holiday camp? The only reason you're still here is to work. Now –

The **Man** *dresses* **Pinocchio** *in a clown's hat and gets a ring – the type that dogs jump through.*

Man   Right. It's about time you worked for your keep. Jump.

Pinocchio *is put through his paces jumping through the hoop. The* **Man** *whips him harder and harder as the hoop gets higher and higher. The* **Man** *screams abuse at* **Pinocchio**. **Pinocchio** *whimpers – he is frightened and exhausted.*

Man   I think you've got the hang of it. Any monkey business and you're straight to the knacker's yard.

The **Man** *blows a whistle and children run in to see the circus. Circus music plays and there is general excitement.*

PINOCCHIO AT THE CIRCUS

Then sudden darkness, then spot on the **Man**, *who plays the role of ringmaster.*

Man   Ladies and Gentlemen, boys and girls. Here, appearing for the very first time, that jumping bean of the asinine world, the one and only Pinocchio, the leaping ass of Lombardy.

Applause. Spotlight on **Pinocchio**. *He is whipped and put through his paces. He is forced to jump higher and higher. He is frightened, exhausted and humiliated. Just as he prepares to make a really big leap he sees a face in the crowd. While everyone else is laughing, the face is sullen and sad. It is the little* **Girl**. *She is almost in tears.*

Pinocchio (*aside*)   It's the little girl. (*As he turns to her his voice becomes a donkey's.*) Hee-haw! Hee-haw!

Pinocchio *tries to run to her.*

Pinocchio   Please help meyore! Hee-haw!

Pinocchio *pleads at the feet of the little* **Girl** *but then the whip cracks and the* **Man** *drags him back to centre stage, beating him as he goes.* **Pinocchio** *looks back to the little* **Girl**, *but she has disappeared. The whip cracks again and he runs to make his leap, but he is hopeless and broken. He throws himself at the hoop but falls horribly, breaking his leg. The little* **Girl** *turns and leaves.*

Pinocchio *writhes around in agony, hee-hawing.*

Man   Get up.

Pinocchio   Hee-haw.

Man   Get up.

It's obvious **Pinocchio** *can't get up.*

Man   This is your last chance.

The **Man** *kicks* **Pinocchio**'s *bad leg. He winces.*

Man   I'm warning you.

Pinocchio *can't get up. The* **Man** *smiles at the audience.*

Man   Ladies and Gentlemen. The marvellous Pinocchio!

Lights out. **Everybody** *is gone, except the* **Man** *and* **Pinocchio**. *His mood is very different now as he scowls at* **Pinocchio** *lying on the ground.*

The **Man** *snaps.*

Man   Right. You're good to no one lame.

He ties a rope round **Pinocchio***'s neck.*

Man   You know what I'm going to do with you? I'm going to make you pay your way. I'm gonna skin your hide and make a nice drum out of you.

The **Man** *drags* **Pinocchio** *across the stage.*

Man   But first I'm gonna have to drown you.

Pinocchio *is squeaking in terror. The* **Man** *drags* **Pinocchio** *nearer and nearer to the front of the stage as if it were a cliff. The* **Man** *looks out.*

Man   If I was you I'd make your peace with your maker 'cos you're going in there. I'll fish you out tomorrow when you're good and bloated.

The **Man** *ties a huge stone to the other end of* **Pinocchio***'s rope.* **Pinocchio** *pleads in donkey language.*

Man   Doesn't make any difference to me, you dumb ass. Say goodbye.

The **Man** *takes the rock and drops it off the edge of the stage. The rope goes tight and* **Pinocchio** *tumbles after it.*

Man   Pity.

The **Man** *lights a cigar.*

Man   Two down. A hundred and fifty-seven to go.

He smiles malevolently into the audience and goes off.

PINOCCHIO IS THROWN INTO THE SEA AND EATEN BY A WHALE

The sea.
Pinocchio *falls into the sea (perhaps the puppet falls on a wire from the flies). He drops down and down. He's washed about and soon fish come and eat away his donkey skin / ears / etc. Or they might dissolve in*

the water. He nearly drowns but once he is rid of his donkey nature he is free to swim up to the surface, but has to lose his rock or is forced to swim with it to the surface -a gargantuan effort. Anyway, lazzo of losing the donkey characteristics and nearly drowning. After a huge effort he reaches the surface and takes a huge breath.

Pinocchio *begins to swim for the shore. He shouts for help. Gradually the waves get stronger and stronger, and buffet him around. He tries to swim against them but they knock him back. He swims with all his might, and escapes the big waves and gets into much calmer water. He starts to luxuriate, swimming around easily and relaxing.*

'Jaws' music.

Just when all is well, the whale appears. **Pinocchio** *sees it and panics. He starts to swim away with incredible speed, but the whale gives chase. Lazzo of the whale chase. (Maybe he sees the hallucination of the little* **Girl***, maybe not if it takes away the tension of the scene.) He narrowly escapes getting eaten several times. The audience are kept on a knife edge. But finally the huge mouth bears down.* **Pinocchio** *tries to get away . . . first he succeeds but, hard as he tries, we see the huge jaws closing in on him as he swims for dear life. The whale snaps his jaws closed.*

Blackout.

PINOCCHIO IS REUNITED WITH GEPPETTO

Inside the whale.

Wheezing. Maybe **Pinocchio** *has some matches from lighting the cigarette. He lights a match to see around him. He is in the belly of the whale. There is a sticky sucking as he walks. He lights a match and looks around. He realises he's trapped.*

Pinocchio   Help! Help! Somebody help!

Pinocchio *makes his way through the innards of the whale. It is an arduous journey. He splishes and splashes, then he spots* **Geppetto** *who is eating a dinner of fish, or perhaps fishing.*

Pinocchio   Hello. Who's there?

Geppetto   Go away. Leave me alone.

Pinocchio   I know that voice. Daddy! I thought you were dead. It's me, Pinocchio.

A moving reunion. **Geppetto** *hugs* **Pinocchio**. *He can barely speak for emotion.*

Geppetto   What are you doing here?

Pinocchio   I came to find you.

They hug.

Pinocchio   O dear, dear Father. I've found you at last. I'll never leave you again, never, ever again.

Geppetto   I can't believe it. Pinocchio. It really is you.

Pinocchio   Yes, yes, it's me! Papa! Oh, please say you forgive me, won't you. I mean, you're such a good father. And if you only knew the misfortunes that have befallen me you'd forgive me right away.

Geppetto   But what happened, Pinocchio?

Pinocchio   Well, first I was born and then you sent me to school . . .

Geppetto   Pinocchio, it doesn't matter. You're here now.

Pinocchio   How long have you been inside the whale, Papa?

Geppetto   Since the day I left to find you. Maybe it's two years, Pinocchio, it feels like two centuries.

Pinocchio   But how have you survived?

Geppetto   Luckily the whale swallowed the entire contents of a sinking cargo ship – so for a while I lived the life of Riley. But you can get very sick of fish. And this is all I have left, Pinocchio. I'm down to my last candle.

Pinocchio   But what will happen now, Father?

Geppetto   We will have to make do in the dark.

Pinocchio   We can't do that. There's no time to lose. We have to get out of here right away.

Geppetto   How, Pinocchio?

Pinocchio   I don't know. By escaping. We'll have to crawl out of the whale's mouth.

Geppetto   I can't do that, Pinocchio, not with my bad back. Besides, I can't even swim.

Pinocchio   You won't have to swim. Just get on my shoulders and I'll take you.

Geppetto   You're dreaming, son. You couldn't carry me. I'm weak. I'm starving.

Pinocchio   Look here.

Pinocchio *finds in his pocket a half-eaten pear.*

Pinocchio   Eat it. It'll give you strength.

Geppetto *looks at the pear and takes it (in a echo of the earlier scene).*

Geppetto   Look, you go. Escape while you have the chance. Just leave me here. I'm finished, Pinocchio.

Pinocchio   Papa, I can't leave you here.

Geppetto   I'd only be a burden. You have your whole life to lead. I'm an old man. My time's up, Pinocchio. I'll stay here and die. Go. Goodbye, my son.

Pinocchio *looks sadly at* **Geppetto**. **Geppetto** *has made his decision.* **Pinocchio** *trembles.* **Geppetto** *kisses* **Pinocchio** *for the last time – then pushes him away, urging him to go.*

Geppetto   I love you, Pinocchio.

Pinocchio *is stunned.*

Geppetto   Go. Please. While you still have a chance.

Pinocchio *hesitates.*

Pinocchio   No, you must come.

Pinocchio *grabs* **Geppetto's** *hand.* **Geppetto** *resists.*

Geppetto   No. Leave me.

Pinocchio   I can't leave you; you have to come.

They struggle. Then **Pinocchio** *pulls* **Geppetto** *along with him.*

Pinocchio   Come on. This way.

The little puppet pulls the big man on a perilous path through the whale. They climb and struggle. Deluges of water sweep them back. It is a huge struggle for the puppet to pull **Geppetto** *with him but on no account will he let go.*

Lazzo of the escape, an arduous journey.

Either as in the book they finally reach the mouth and look out at the night sky, or seeing we have done all the talking, like the improvisation, they should be finding it very difficult to escape but finally they are blown out by the whale and they tumble into the fomenting brine.

PINOCCHIO TRIES TO SAVE GEPPETTO IN THE SEA

The sea.

Geppetto *starts to sink but* **Pinocchio** *won't let go. He swims for dear life, but* **Geppetto** *is too heavy. A struggle against the element to save* **Geppetto**.

Pinocchio *manages to save* **Geppetto** *and get him back to the surface, when the sea gets the better of them and sweeps them away.*

The waves subside and **Pinocchio** *and* **Geppetto** *are left washed up on the beach.* **Geppetto** *gradually gets up, he sees* **Pinocchio** *lying there. He rushes to him.* **Pinocchio** *is limp and lifeless. It seems this time he really has died.*

Geppetto   Pinocchio. My Pinocchio.

Then **Pinocchio** *gradually wakes up. But he has a more mature voice. He grabs* **Geppetto**.

Pinocchio   You're alive.

Pinocchio *suddenly realises his movements are not jerky any more, but human-like.*

Pinocchio   Papa, Papa. Can you see? (*He gets up and moves sinuously.*) Papa. I'm a real boy.

Pinocchio *starts to cry gently, withholding any big emotion.*

Pinocchio (sadly)   I'm a boy.

Geppetto *looks at him. Both are in awe of the transformation, but completely aware of its gravity. The frivolity of puppethood and childishness have been shed.*

The stage is silent.

Pinocchio (*in the manner of a grown man, softly*)   I'm a boy.

Blackout.

Spot on a trapdoor. It opens – the **Cat**. *Very battered. She holds out a begging bowl.*

Cat   Please spare something for a blind, homeless feline.

A chord.

Spot on the other trap door. It opens – the **Fox**.

Fox   Please help us. We're homeless, brainless and hungry.

Music starts. It is up-tempo and frivolous compared with the subdued transformation scene.

Final Song

> I'm a Boy, I'm a Boy,
> Oh, it's great to be a Boy;
> I'm a Boy, I'm a Boy,
> Oh, it's great to be a Boy.

I will never get my feet burnt,
I will never sit inside a whale,
I will always do my homework; you
Will see I'll never fail.

I will always help my father.
I will learn to tootle on the flute.
I will always eat bananas and
All kinds of healthy fruit.

I'm a Boy, I'm a Boy,
Oh, it's great to be a Boy;
I'm a Boy, I'm a Boy,
Oh, Oh, it's great to be a Boy.

I will say my prayers at night time.
I'll learn algebra all of the day.
I will be nice to the homeless, I'll
Give all my things away.

I think I will get married and
then I will get divorced,
And everyone will laugh and smile and
No one will be forced.

I'm a Boy, I'm a Boy,
Oh, it's great to be a Boy,
I'm a Boy, I'm a Boy,
Oh, Oh, it's great to be a Boy.

I will save the world from ruin;
I will save the world from every sin;
I'll kill everyone that's evil;
I will always wear a grin.

We all will live for ever more.
We will never, ever, ever die.
We will live off bits of pastry and
The crusts of apple pie.

I'm a Boy, I'm a Boy,
Oh, it's great to be a Boy;
I'm a Boy, I'm a Boy,
Oh, Oh, it's great to be a Boy.

No more death or hardship,
There'll be no tears or woe or pain.
We will live the life of Riley
And it will never ever rain.

Lights out.